ENGLISH BY NEWSPAPER

How to Read and Understand an English Language Newspaper

Terry L. Fredrickson
University of Minnesota

Paul F. Wedel
United Press International

HEINLE & HEINLE PUBLISHERS
A Division of Wadsworth, Inc.
Boston, Massachusetts 02116

Library of Congress Cataloging in Publication Data

Fredrickson, Terry L.
  English by newspaper.

  1. English language--Text-books for foreign speakers.
2. Readers--Journalism.   3. Readers--Current events.
4. Newspapers in education.   I. Wedel, Paul F.   II. Title.
PE1128.F675   1984   428.6'4   83-19464

Cover and interior book design by Sally Carson

ISBN 0-8384-2996-3

First printing: January 1984

Printed in the U.S.A.

13 14

Introduction

English by Newspaper gives you a skill that you can use to improve your English for the rest of your life: the ability to read and understand an English language newspaper.

- This book contains:
  1. A reading comprehension method that you can use for almost any nonfiction reading—not just the newspaper.
  2. Exercises that give you practice in using this method.
  3. Specially designed news stories that cover most of the subjects commonly found in your English language newspaper.
  4. A glossary of essential newspaper vocabulary.
  5. An appendix that gives the answers to the exercises.

- You will learn to:
  1. Catch the main idea of a story.
  2. Understand the all-important opening sentence of a news story.
  3. Find the story's essential details.
  4. Use the story to guess the meanings of new words.
  5. Understand newspaper headlines.
  6. Read a news story critically.
  7. Understand newspaper features and editorials.

How to Use This Book

- Six Important Suggestions:
  1. Look over the whole book before you begin.
  2. Note that some words are printed in *italics*. These words are often found in the newspaper and their meanings are explained in the glossary in the back of the book. The words in the glossary are defined according to how they are used in the stories. For this reason, some of the definitions may differ from those you might find in a dictionary.
  3. *English by Newspaper* is most effective when used together with an actual newspaper. When you learn a new method, try it out with an English language newspaper and see how well it works. When you finish a section from the sample stories, try to find a similar story in a recent newspaper. You will be surprised how many words you recognize.

4. Work regularly. A little every day is better than a lot once a week or once a month. With regular reading you should see much improvement within a short time.

5. *English by Newspaper* has an answer key. This means you can choose to work without a teacher. However, you should try not to use the answer key until you have made your best effort to do an exercise by yourself. Studies have proven that people learn more if they work out a problem before they know the correct answer.

6. Do not overuse the glossary. The glossary is very convenient and tempting to use, but it is important to try to understand as much of a story as you can without it.

To the Teacher

Here are seven reasons why teachers around the world use the English language newspaper as an essential part of their reading programs:

1. It is a source of up-to-the-minute English.
2. It covers subjects of immediate interest and importance.
3. It is an excellent tool for building vocabulary.
4. It is readily available and can even be delivered to your doorstep.
5. Its consistent style and content make it one of the easiest reading materials written for native speakers.
6. Since most students already have a background in current affairs from local language newspapers, radio, and television, it can be introduced before other types of unsimplified materials.
7. It is the one type of English reading material that students are most likely to continue reading after they complete their education.

The English language newspaper is an attractive possibility for almost any reading comprehension program. Unlike most other reading materials, it can be taught as a coherent unit. It is not a loose collection of stories varying widely in style and content. The teacher can be confident that what is learned from one story can be quickly applied to another. In addition, it is a medium that lends itself splendidly to strategies fostered in progressive reading programs—skimming, scanning, anticipation, the use of context, vocabulary development, inference, and critique.

All this because newspaper journalism, especially the hard news variety, is predictable. A story is summarized at the beginning and then retold in greater detail. Items are arranged in descending order of importance. Sentence structure is highly consistent and vocabulary is largely topic specific—fire has one set of high-frequency terms, election results have another. Technical terms are explained.

This predictability can be exploited and *English By Newspaper* points the way. The book presents a systematic approach to the English language newspaper, providing a thoroughly tested reading comprehension method and an overview of the topics and vocabulary most commonly encountered. It can be used as the core reference book for a newspaper course or as a supplementary text for a more general reading comprehension course. It is designed to be a self-study program, so classroom time can be spent applying the method to actual newspaper stories.

Here are some suggestions:

1. If at all possible, use *English By Newspaper* in conjunction with a newspaper. Most English language newspapers have discount rates for students and many offer special limited subscriptions, allowing for perhaps a single delivery a week. The use of old issues is another possibility. Newspaper companies are often willing to give away multiple copies of newspapers returned from newsstands. If you use this alternative, try to obtain several consecutive issues, so you can follow the development of major stories.

2. Tape radio or TV broadcasts of the day's news and use them as listening comprehension exercises to supplement the newspaper. Compare the newspaper's treatment of a story with that of a weekly news magazine.

3. Design activities that build on the knowledge your students have gained from the newspaper. If, for example, you read about a major strike, divide the class into workers and management and have a debate based on newspaper accounts of their positions. This is not only entertaining, but it activates vocabulary that might otherwise remain passive.

4. Follow major stories. Note that each story has a core vocabulary that is repeated day after day. Discuss the stories thoroughly and have the students try to anticipate future developments. This will give them a reason to open tomorrow's newspaper and will increase their comprehension as well.

Credits

The excerpts from AP, UPI and Reuters news stories were reprinted by permission.

The authors wish to thank United Press International for the photographs appearing in this book on pages 6, 23, 36, 51, 69, 72, 86, 95, 106, 117, 124, and 126.

The authors also wish to thank the following organizations for photographs: Stock, Boston, Inc. (Charles Gatewood): cover photo; French Embassy, New York: p. 113; and Seabrook Station Education Center: p. 133.

Contents

PART ONE: A READING COMPREHENSION METHOD

PART TWO: HIGH-FREQUENCY NEWS STORIES

An overview of the topics most commonly found in the English language newspaper, Part Two contains specially written news stories which include much of the vocabulary necessary for understanding the newspaper. All stories are followed by comprehension questions.

ENGLISH
BY NEWSPAPER

A Reading
Comprehension Method

Scanning

This chapter will show you how to use your present knowledge of English to understand the main ideas of a newspaper story without using a dictionary.

To scan is to make a quick first reading of the story. This has three purposes:
1. To find out what the story is about.
2. To find out whether the story interests you.
3. To get a quick general understanding of a story you have chosen to read.

(A) Focusing on the Beginning

You will usually find the most important point of a news story in the first paragraph (called "the lead"), so this is the place to begin your scanning. Look for words you understand. Two or three key words will often be enough to catch the main idea.

Hanoi rages over spying charges

HONG KONG (Reuter)—<u>Vietnam</u> yesterday angrily rejected <u>American</u> charges that Vietnamese diplomats were involved in espionage and warned that such accusations could jeopardize US attempts to normalize relations.

This is clearly a story about Vietnam and the United States. From the word **angrily** you can be quite sure that it must report some

3

problem between the two countries. This is enough for successful scanning. If the subject doesn't interest you, scan other stories until you find one that does.

EXERCISE

Read the following newspaper leads. Look for key words that you already understand. Then answer the questions that follow. Note that the key words are underlined for you in the first three stories. You should finish each item in less than a minute. You can check your answers on page 161 in the appendix.

1.

Battle over Narita Airport

NARITA, Japan (Reuter)—Red-helmeted students and more than 800 riot police yesterday fought running battles for the second consecutive day to gain control of a concrete and steel tower at Tokyo's controversial new international airport.

This story is about:
   a. the completion of a new airport in Tokyo.
   b. a fight between students and police at a Tokyo airport.
   c. the building of a concrete and steel tower at Tokyo's international airport.

I AM / AM NOT interested in reading this story.

2.

Defector weds

NEW YORK (Reuter)—A top-ranking Soviet diplomat, who defected from his United Nations post and later became embroiled in a controversy over payments to a professional escort girl, has secretly married an American woman, Newsweek magazine reported yesterday.

This story is about:
   a. a problem in the United Nations.
   b. a marriage between a Russian man and an American woman.
   c. a secret agreement between Russia and the United States.

I AM / AM NOT interested in reading this story.

4

3.

Rich find in Ireland

DUBLIN (Reuter)—A hoard of Eighth Century treasure, including a priceless silver and gold chalice, has been found in an Irish bog, the Government announced Thursday.

This story is about:
    a. the Irish economy.
    b. the price of silver and gold.
    c. the finding of treasure.

I AM / AM NOT interested in reading this story.

4.

Diplomat leaps to freedom

BOGOTA, Colombia (UPI)—Uruguayan Ambassador Fernando Gómez leaped out of a window of the besieged Dominican Embassy early yesterday in a dramatic escape from leftist guerrillas who are holding 19 other diplomats captive.

This story is about:
    a. an escape.
    b. a visit.
    c. an election.

I AM / AM NOT interested in reading this story.

5.

Death threats to Fondas

LOS ANGELES (Reuter)—A 31-year-old man was arrested here Saturday on suspicion of making death threats to film star Henry Fonda and his children, Jane and Peter Fonda.

This story is about:
    a. an arrest.
    b. a murder.
    c. film stars on holiday in Los Angeles.

I AM / AM NOT interested in reading this story.

6.

UK-France iron out problems

PARIS (Reuter)—French President Valery Giscard d'Estaing arrived in Britain for talks with Prime Minister Margaret Thatcher on major differences between the two countries over EEC policies.

This story is about:
    a. an agreement.
    b. a United Nations meeting.
    c. a visit.

I AM / AM NOT interested in reading this story.

7.

UK steel industry shuts down

LONDON (UPI)—Britain's state-owned steelworks shut down at midnight last night in the first nationwide steel strike since 1926, threatening widespread disruption of Britain's heavy industries.

This story is about:
    a. British steel production in 1926.
    b. a steel strike.
    c. rebuilding Britain's steelworks.

I AM / AM NOT interested in reading this story.

New light shed on Kennedy shooting?

WASHINGTON (Reuter)—A new theory that four shots, not three, may have been fired when President Kennedy was assassinated is being studied in an attempt to show that Lee Harvey Oswald, his accused assassin, did not act alone.

This story is about:
   a. the killing of President Kennedy.
   b. the opening of the Kennedy Center in Washington.
   c. President Kennedy's large family.
I AM / AM NOT interested in reading this story.

Now try this method with an English language newspaper or with several of the stories in the back of this book. Do not be unhappy if you are not always able to understand the subject of a story. Your vocabulary may not be big enough. If you are diligent, however, you will see a big improvement from week to week and month to month. In fact, by the time you finish this book you will be able to catch the main idea of almost any story—just from scanning.

(B) Scanning the Entire Story

When you have found an interesting story, you should read quickly through it. You are scanning the entire story in much the same way you scanned the lead—to find out as many important facts as you can without using a dictionary. This will give you a general understanding of the story which will help you greatly when you go back and read the story more carefully.

In section A you scanned a story about the finding of a treasure. Here is the complete story. Read through it quickly and see how many important facts you can discover in two minutes.

Rich find in Ireland

DUBLIN (Reuter)—A hoard of Eighth Century treasure, including a priceless silver and gold chalice, has been found in an Irish bog, the Government announced Thursday.

It is regarded as the most significant Irish archeological and historical find this century and was uncovered about two weeks ago by an amateur with a metal detector, government officials said.

The finder and precise location of the burial place, somewhere in County Tipperary in the Irish Midlands, are being kept secret, Brian O'Riordain, Director of the National Museum of Ireland, told reporters.

It has not yet been worked out when (Continued on next page)

(Continued from p. 7)
the objects were buried, but museum officials speculated that they might have been hidden by a monk or priest to protect them from plunder by Vikings.

The hoard has been acquired by the Government as a treasure trove, but there would probably be a reward for the finder.

It was found in bogland near a river but no other details are being released until further archeological work has been carried out.

The collection has been sent to the British Museum for cleaning and restoration and will then go on display in the National Museum of Ireland, museum officials said.

You should have been able to find out the following:

Q: What kind of treasure was found?
A: A silver and gold chalice and other unmentioned items.
Q: Who found it?
A: An unnamed amateur.
Q: Where was it found?
A: Somewhere in Ireland.
Q: When was it found?
A: Two weeks ago.
Q: Where is it now?
A: In the British Museum.

Note that the questions were answered only in a general way. You can add specific details later. It is also unnecessary to understand all the vocabulary at this time.

EXERCISE

Scan the following and answer the questions. Try to use no more than two minutes for each story.

1.

UK steel industry shuts down

LONDON (UPI)—Britain's state-owned steelworks shut down at midnight last night in the first nationwide steel strike since 1926, threatening widespread disruption of Britain's heavy industries.

Final hopes of averting the strike failed on Monday when unions and management refused to budge from their positions on steelworkers' pay.

"The strike is on. It is an impossibility to call it off. The only question now is how long it lasts," said Bill Sirs, leader of the steelworkers' Union.

The steelworkers are demanding a 20 percent pay increase but the employers are sticking to their offer of six percent on basic rates.

This story is about:
a. British steel production in 1926.
b. a steel strike.
c. rebuilding Britain's steelworks.

How big a pay increase do the workers want?
    a. 20 percent   b. six percent   c. The story doesn't say.

How big a pay increase is management willing to give?
    a. 20 percent   b. six percent   c. The story doesn't say.

2.

Saved from tar pit

LOS ANGELES (AP)—Rescue workers formed a human chain to save the life of a 24-year-old man who plunged into the La Brea tar pits, a graveyard of prehistoric animals, in an apparent suicide attempt, officials say.

Bruce Remy, who was totally immersed except for his face and one hand, escaped without injuries Sunday. But he had to spend four hours in the emergency room while Cedars-Sinai Hospital workers scrubbed him clean with mineral oil.

Police spokesman sergeant Jim Richart said Remy apparently was trying to kill himself when he entered the 10-meter-diameter pit, one of the smallest at the county park. The pits of gooey tar have preserved the bones of prehistoric dinosaurs.

Remy told firefighters he was grateful that they had saved his life.

This story is about:
    a. a rescue.
    b. the finding of a prehistoric animal.
    c. the opening of a new graveyard.

Who was saved?
    a. A prehistoric animal.
    b. Bruce Remy.
    c. Jim Richart.

Was he hurt?
    a. Yes, he was.   b. No, he wasn't.   c. The story doesn't say.

What was he trying to do?
    a. to steal a prehistoric animal.
    b. to dig a grave.
    c. to kill himself.

3.

Portugal fire out of control

LOUSA SIERRA, Portugal (UPI)—Busloads of soldiers and volunteers have joined the fight against a 20-km-wide forest fire that threatens the homes of 1,200 villagers northeast of Lisbon.

(Continued on next page)

(Continued from p. 9)
The fire, which raged uncontrolled early yesterday, is the latest in a series of blazes to hit southern Europe this month, killing 29 people.

The villages of Alges and Torno in the Lousa Sierra region 240 km northeast of Lisbon lay directly in the track of a 20-km fire front and were "in extreme danger" Tuesday night, said firefighter Jorge Carlos Fernandes.

Officials said they suspected arson when the fire began Sunday. The blaze was believed under control Monday, but flared anew and four busloads of soldiers and volunteers joined the fight Tuesday.

The firefighters, estimated at 800 people, were backed by amphibious planes and helicopters until dusk when the aircraft were grounded.

This story is about:
    a. a Portuguese village.
    b. a fight between soldiers and volunteers.
    c. a forest fire in Portugal.
How many people were killed?
    a. 20   b. 29   c. 1200
Where did the event happen?
    a. 20 kilometers from Lousa Sierra.
    b. 1,200 kilometers northeast of Lisbon.
    c. 240 kilometers northeast of Lisbon.
Who was in the fight?
    a. soldiers and volunteers.
    b. planes and helicopters.
    c. both of the above.

4.

Briton off on bid to set flying record

LOS ANGELES (Reuter)—British insurance broker David Springbett took off from here Tuesday night on the first leg of his attempt to fly around the world aboard commercial airliners in a record 46 hours.

Carrying a suitcase containing three clean shirts, a toothbrush and a copy of the ABC World Airways Guide in case he has to find alternative routes, Springbett, 41, left aboard a British Airways 747 jumbo jet for his first stop, London.

After staying up 13 hours here on Tuesday so he could sleep on the planes, Springbett will fly aboard a British Airways Concorde Supersonic airliner from London to Singapore and then return here by way of Bangkok, Manila, Tokyo and Honolulu.

"I'm doing this partly to give a boost to Concorde, partly to show airliners generally keep time and simply for the hell of it," said Springbett, whose air ticket cost $8,000.

There are faster ways of flying here from Singapore, but Springbett said under the rules of the International Avia-
(Continued on next page)

(Continued from p. 10)
tion Federation he must travel at least the distance of the Tropic of Cancer, 22,858 miles (37,787 km), to claim the record. Springbett said the present record was set by two Australian journalists, Terry Sloane and Alec Prior, who flew round the world aboard scheduled airliners from Sydney in March, 1978, in 53 hours and 34 minutes.

This story is about:
    a. an attempt to set a record for traveling around the world.
    b. selling insurance to the world's airlines.
    c. inexpensive around-the-world holiday tours.

What is David Springbett's goal?
    a. to make his trip in 46 hours.
    b. to earn $8,000.
    c. to find the most convenient route around the world for tourists.

What is the present record?
    a. 53 hours and 34 minutes.
    b. 22,858 miles.
    c. London to Singapore in 13 hours.

Now scan stories either from the sample stories at the back of this book or from an English language newspaper.

CHAPTER

The Newspaper Lead

In this chapter you will learn how to read the most important paragraph of a news story—the first one.

The first paragraph of a news story is called the lead. It almost always gives you the story's main topic and most important facts.

The lead is like all English sentences. It is built around the subject and main verb. If you can find them, you have a good start toward understanding the lead sentence and the whole story.

In the following example, note how the rest of the sentence only adds information to the subject and main verb.

* Example:

Subject and main verb:	**A bus fell.**
Additional Information:	
Where did the bus fall?	A bus fell **into a lake near Montreal.**
When did it fall?	A bus fell into a lake near Montreal **late yesterday.**
What was the result?	A bus fell into a lake near Montreal late yesterday, **killing 41 of the 48 persons aboard.**
What caused the bus to fall?	An **out-of-control** bus fell into a lake near Montreal late yesterday, killing 41 of the 48 persons aboard.
Who was inside?	An out-of-control bus, **carrying a group of mentally-retarded and handicapped people,** fell into a lake near Montreal late yesterday, killing 41 of the 48 persons aboard.
Where was the bus going and where was it coming from?	An out-of-control bus, carrying a group of mentally-retarded and handicapped people **home from a**

What kind of a bus was it?

theater outing, fell into a lake near Montreal late yesterday, killing 41 of the 48 persons aboard.

An out-of-control **charter** bus, carrying a group of mentally-retarded and handicapped people home from a theater outing, fell into a lake yesterday, killing 41 of the 48 persons aboard.

In the actual lead the writer made one small change, using the word "hurtled" instead of "fell" to indicate that the bus was moving at great speed. Here is the complete sentence as it appeared in newspapers around the world.

> MONTREAL (UPI)—An out-of-control charter bus, carrying a group of mentally-retarded and handicapped people home from a theater outing, hurtled into a lake near Montreal late yesterday, killing 41 of the 48 persons aboard.

This is a great deal of information in a single sentence. Do you see how the writer has organized the sentence around the subject and main verb?

	SUBJECT	
—charter	**a bus**	—carrying a group of mentally-retarded and handicapped people
—out-of-control		—home from a theater outing
	MAIN VERB	
	hurtled	Where? —into a lake near Montreal
		When? —late yesterday
		Result? —killing 41 of the 48 persons aboard.

(A) Finding the Subject and the Main Verb

In many stories the subject and the main verb come at the very beginning of the sentence.

China has cut . . .

The Government has announced . . .

Doctors will operate . . .

Sometimes the newspaper writer adds description and puts one or more adjectives in front of the subject.

Australian scientists say . . .

A young factory worker was killed . . .

A 31-year-old German tourist was jailed . . .

13

The writer may have to give even more information about the subject. The writer does this by putting the information after the subject and before the main verb.

> William Clohan, who was fired last week as under-secretary of education, said Tuesday he believes he was ousted because of right-wing pressure on the White House.

Such sentences are usually easy to recognize for two reasons:
1. The descriptive information is often set apart by commas.

> Delbert Wilson, who authored more than fifty books for young children and teenagers, died yesterday at the age of fifty-seven.
>
> Raydel Carrington, an announcer for WBBM-TV, was found shot in the stomach early Thursday, police said.
>
> Chancellor Helmut Schmidt, in an apparent attempt to give a sense of new activity and ideas to his government, will announce Cabinet changes, including a new finance minister, in the next few days.

2. Even if there are no commas to help you, the subject is often followed by a clause beginning with the words **who, which,** or **that**.

> More than forty people who attempted to block vehicles from entering a nuclear power plant were arrested Tuesday.
>
> A storm which dumped more than four inches of rain in Kansas Friday moved into the Ohio Valley, threatening residents with flash floods.
>
> A new law that prescribes harsh punishment for drunken drivers goes into effect today.

EXERCISE

Find the subject and main verb in each of the following and answer the questions. The first one has been done for you. (Meanings of the *italicized* words can be found in the glossary.)

14

1.

> LONDON (Reuter)—John Stonehouse, former British cabinet *minister* who faked his own death by drowning, was freed from jail on *parole* yesterday after serving three years for *theft, fraud* and *deception.*

Subject: *John Stonehouse*   Main Verb: *was freed*

This story is about:

   a. a drowning.

   (b.) the freeing of a man from jail.

   c. a theft.

2.

> JOHANNESBURG (Reuter)—A 20-year-old woman who was to have married her step-grandfather in Johannesburg Friday was told by a *magistrate* a few minutes before the ceremony that the marriage was *illegal.*

Subject: Main Verb:

This story is about:

   a. a marriage.

   b. a magistrate's decision.

   c. an illegal ceremony.

3.

> COUNCIL BLUFFS, Iowa (AP)—An explosion that may have been caused by grain dust ripped apart a grain elevator Tuesday, throwing *debris* up to a mile away, killing five people and injuring at least 22.

Subject: Main Verb:

This story is about:

   a. an explosion.

   b. a dust storm.

   c. a battle in a war.

A possible cause for the accident was:

   a. grain dust.

   b. debris.

   c. a grain elevator.

4.

> BEIRUT, Lebanon (Reuter)—Iraq, in the hope of getting peace *negotiations* started, announced today that the last of its soldiers had left Iran.

Subject: Main Verb:

This story is about:

   a. peace negotiations.

   b. Iranian soldiers.

   c. an Iraqi announcement.

5. | LONDON (Reuter)—A crippling transport strike *threatened* Britain yesterday with food shortages, soaring *unemployment* and a virtual shutdown of industry. |

Subject: Main Verb:

This story is about:
   a. British transportation.
   b. a strike.
   c. unemployment in Britain.

6. | LONDON (UPI)—The remote Scottish island of Iona, the birthplace of Christianity in Britain and the resting place of 48 Scottish kings, has been bought for the nation for 1.5 million. |

Subject: Main Verb:

This story is about:
   a. Christianity in Britain.
   b. 48 Scottish kings.
   c. the buying of an island.

7. | PANAMA CITY (AP)—About 130 Panamanians who battled alongside Sandinista *guerrillas* in Nicaragua returned home Friday to a hero's welcome. |

Subject: Main Verb:

This story is about:
   a. a battle between Sandinista guerrillas and Panama.
   b. a battle between Panama and Nicaragua.
   c. a return home.

8. | LOS ANGELES (Reuter)—Christopher Boyce, one of the so-called "dishonorable schoolboys" who supplied US *spy satellite* secrets to the Soviet Union, has escaped from a minimum security prison at Lompoc. |

Subject: Main Verb:

This story is about:
   a. a dishonest schoolboy.
   b. spy satellite secrets.
   c. an escape from prison.

Who is Christopher Boyce?
   a. a schoolboy.
   b. a person who gave secrets to the Soviet Union.
   c. a Russian prisoner.

16

$\textcircled{B}$ *A Problem Sentence*

Try to find the main verb in the following sentence:

> A woman said to be despondent over her husband's
> heavy drinking jumped into a canal with her three
> children late Friday.

The main verb is **jumped**—not **said**. The woman in the story didn't say anything at all. Someone else said that she was very unhappy about her husband's heavy drinking causing her to jump into the canal.

Leaving Out Understood Words

In English, it is sometimes possible to leave out the first words of a clause that follows a noun. Most often these missing words will be **who** (or **which**) and a form of the verb **be**. This is what happened in the preceding example. If we put back the missing words, the sentence reads:

> A woman <u>who was</u> said to be despondent over her
> husband's heavy drinking, jumped into a canal with
> her three children late Friday.

It is quite easy to mistake the first verb in such sentences for the main verb and thereby misunderstand the story. When you read these sentences, therefore, you cannot translate word by word. You must keep reading until you are sure that you have found the main verb.

Read the following examples carefully and look for clues that help you see that the first verb is not the main verb.

EXAMPLE 1

> A California man attempting to cross the Atlantic
> Ocean in a rowboat radioed Tuesday that he has
> passed the halfway point and "all is well."

Attempting could not possibly be the main verb. A verb + "ing" must follow a form of the verb "be." The main verb in this sentence is "radioed." If we fill in the missing words, the sentence reads:

> A California man <u>who is</u> attempting to cross the
> Atlantic Ocean in a rowboat radioed Tuesday that he
> had passed the halfway point and "all is well."

EXAMPLE 2

> Police led by dogs captured an escaped convict Saturday, deep in a Connecticut forest.

Most verbs in shortened clauses are in the passive voice. For this reason, many of these clauses contain a phrase beginning with the word **by**. This phrase tells who or what did the action that is described in the clause. Note the passive voice verb and the **by** phrase in the following sentence:

> Police <u>who were led by dogs</u> captured an escaped convict Saturday, deep in a Connecticut forest.

EXAMPLE 3

> An ancient ship discovered near Lake Ontario may be of Viking origin.

Example 3 is similar to example 2, although there is no **by** phrase to help you see that the verb is in the passive voice. If you think about the meaning, however, the verb **discovered** must be in the passive voice. A ship is not alive and could not discover anything. Filling in the missing words, we get:

> An ancient ship <u>which was</u> discovered near Lake Ontario may be of Viking origin.

EXAMPLE 4

> An Italian magazine published Thursday in Rome claimed that two high Italian military officers gave away NATO defense plans to the Soviets.

In this sentence, there is little to help you see that **published** is not the main verb. Note, however, there is a second verb (**claimed**) which gives the sentence its proper meaning. Always keep reading until you are sure you have found the main verb.

EXERCISE

Find the subject and main verb in each of the following sentences and answer the questions. The first one has been done for you. In this exercise you will find examples of all of the sentences we have discussed so far—not just the problem sentences of this section.

1.

> NEW YORK (UPI)—Firefighters returning to the
> scene of a minor *blaze* yesterday found thousands of
> gallons of highly *toxic* chemicals in an *abandoned*
> Brooklyn manufacturing company.

Subject: Firefighters   Main Verb: found

This story is about:

  a. a small fire.

  (b.) the finding of dangerous chemicals.

  c. a manufacturing company which produces dangerous chemicals.

2.

> CAIRO, Egypt (AP)—Five Muslim *fundamentalists*
> *convicted* of the *assassination* of President Anwar
> Sadat were *executed* early Thursday, hours after a
> *clemency plea* was *rejected* by Hosni Mubarak,
> Sadat's *successor.*

Subject: Main Verb:

This story is about:

  a. the execution of five assassins.

  b. the conviction of five assassins.

  c. the replacement of Anwar Sadat by Hosni Mubarak.

3.

> PARIS (UPI)—Police and fire department *officials*
> sought the cause today of a chain of three explosions in
> a fashionable *residential* area which left five dead and
> more than 40 injured.

Subject: Main Verb:

This story is about:

  a. an attempt to find the cause of three explosions.

  b. the deaths of five people.

  c. a problem between Paris police and the fire department.

4.

> UNITED NATIONS (Reuter)—The first planeload
> of medicines and medical equipment assembled by
> international *relief* agencies was sent to Phnom Penh
> Thursday from Ho Chi Minh City.

Subject: Main Verb:

This story is about:

  a. the assembling of medicines and medical equpment.

  b. the sending of medicines and medical equipment.

  c. the opening of an air route between Phnom Penh and Ho Chi Minh City.

5. | TOKYO (AP)—A Japanese-Chinese from Manchuria, separated from his family since the end of World War II, met his parents in Osaka Thursday in a tearful reunion that coincided with the 33rd anniversary of Japan's *surrender* to the Allied Forces.

Subject: Main Verb:

This story is about:
   a. the reuniting of a man with his parents.
   b. the end of World War II.
   c. the 33rd anniversary of Japan's surrender.

6. | ANNECY, France (AP)—Three French explorers emerged from underground Sunday, exhausted after spending a week trapped on a tiny, frigid ledge about 1,800 feet below the earth's surface.

Subject: Main Verb:

This story is about:
   a. the return of three French explorers.
   b. the deaths of three French explorers.
   c. a holiday below the earth's surface.

7. | SANTA FE, New Mexico (Reuter)—Princess Anne, asked how she felt being an aunt with the birth of a son to her brother, Prince Charles, and the Princess of Wales, told reporters, "That's my business!"

Subject: Main Verb:

This story is about:
   a. the aunt of Prince Charles and the Princess of Wales.
   b. the birth of a prince.
   c. a statement by Princess Anne.

8. | ROME (UPI)—Roaming bands of *ex-convicts* demanding steady work seized 15 city buses in Naples, Italy.

Subject: Main Verb:

This story is about:
   a. a workers' strike.
   b. the seizure of city buses.
   c. a band concert.

9. | NEW YORK (Reuter)—Alger Hiss, the former State Department official who was convicted of *perjury* 28 years ago in one of the most *controversial trials* in American history, has *filed* a court *suit* in an effort to clear his name.

Subject: Main Verb:

This story is about:

     a. the filing of a court suit.

     b. a controversial trial.

     c. the conviction of Alger Hiss.

10. | HOUSTON, Texas (UPI)—A teenager promised a trip to Washington by US Health, Education and Welfare Secretary Joseph Califano if she quit smoking for six months has decided she'd rather smoke than travel.

Subject: Main Verb:

This story is about:

     a. a teenager's promise to quit smoking.

     b. a trip to Washington.

     c. a teenager's decision.

The teenager in the story:

     a. has quit smoking for six months.

     b. has traveled to Washington with Joseph Califano.

     c. has decided not to quit smoking.

Now try to find the subjects and main verbs in stories from an English language newspaper. You can also use stories from the back of this book.

C) *The Rest of the Sentence*

The subject and the main verb are very important, but there are other things you must learn to recognize as well. Here are some of the things a writer can tell you in the rest of the sentence.

1. The writer can **answer questions** about the action stated in the story.

> LONDON (AP)—A massive explosion and fire destroyed [what?] the Italian Consulate [where?] in London's fashionable Belgravia district [when?] early yesterday, [result?] leaving "nothing but a black hole."

2. The writer can **add background** to help you better understand the story.

> LAMIA, Greece (UPI)—The Lamia public prosecutor Saturday indicted the brother and two sisters of Eleni Karyoti, [Who is Eleni Karyoti?] the woman imprisoned in a cellar by her family for 29 years.

> MOUNTAIN VIEW, California (UPI)—A NASA probe of Venus Sunday detected unexpectedly high levels of two primeval gases on the planet, [Why is this important?] a finding that may cause scientists to change their theories on the origin of the solar system.

3. The writer can tell you where he got his information, the **source** of his story.

> STOCKHOLM (AP)—Two Saab Viggen jet fighters of the Swedish Air Force collided in flight Thursday night and crashed in flames, killing at least one of the pilots, <u>an Air Force spokesman said yesterday.</u>

The source is usually mentioned at the end of the story, but if it is very important it comes at the beginning.

> PEKING (AP)—<u>Premier Zhao Aiyang reported a</u> "decisive victory" Monday in streamlining China's central government, but said this was just a beginning toward building an efficient, professional bureaucracy.

EXERCISE

Read each of the following and fill in the necessary information. In this exercise, consider the source to be a complete phrase (for example, "President Reagan said Friday night that").

1.
> BRISBANE (UPI)—A *strike* by power workers *threatened* to cut off all electricity in the state of Queensland yesterday, leaving its 2.5 million *residents* in the dark.

A strike by power workers threatened:
WHAT?
WHERE?
WHEN?
RESULT?

2.
> VATICAN CITY (AP)—The *cardinals* of the Roman Catholic Church yesterday elected 58-year-old Polish Cardinal Karol Wojtyla as *pope*, the first non-Italian in 450 years to be named *pontiff* of the 700-million-member church.

The cardinals of the Roman Catholic Church yesterday elected:
BACKGROUND:
WHOM?
AS WHAT?

3. | LOS ANGELES (Reuter)—Bianca Jagger yesterday
    | *filed for a divorce* from Rolling Stone singer Mick
    | Jagger according to her lawyer.

Bianca Jagger yesterday filed:
FROM WHOM?
SOURCE:
FOR WHAT?

4. | HONG KONG (UPI)—US Rep. Elizabeth Holzman
    | *charged* yesterday that Vietnamese *refugees* have been
    | forced to pay as much as $30 million to the Hanoi
    | Government to win permission to *flee* the country.

Vietnamese refugees have been forced:
HOW MUCH?
TO DO WHAT?
SOURCE:
TO WHOM?
WHY?

5. | LONDON (UPI)—A *controversial bill* to tighten
    | Britain's 12-year-old *abortion* law will come up for
    | final *debate* in the House of Commons today amid
    | outraged *protests* from *feminists* and *politicians* who
    | claim it would drive women to back-street abortionists.

A controversial bill to tighten Britain's 12-year-old abortion law will
come up:
WHEN?
BACKGROUND:
FOR WHAT?

6. ARLINGTON, Oregon (AP)—A father and son have died in a boating accident on the Columbia River, marking the fourth time in four generations that members of the same family have *perished* on the river, relatives said.

A father and son have died:
WHERE?
BACKGROUND:
SOURCE:
HOW?

7. LONDON (UPI)—Jakov Stalin, son of the late Soviet *dictator*, attempted *suicide* in a Nazi *concentration camp* in 1943 by hurling himself onto an electrified barbed wire fence, the Sunday Times said.

Jakov Stalin, son of the late Soviet dictator, attempted:
SOURCE:
HOW?
WHAT?
WHEN?
WHERE?

8. LONDON (Reuter)—The wife of a British *surgeon* has been *sentenced* to 80 lashes in public in Saudi Arabia for breaking the country's strict alcohol laws, the Foreign Office said last night.

The wife of a British surgeon has been sentenced:
WHY?
WHERE?
SOURCE:
TO WHAT?

(D) *Another Common Sentence Pattern*

Some lead sentences begin with a phrase that does not contain the subject. Can you find the main idea of the following story?

WASHINGTON (UPI)—Braving minefields and soldiers with shoot-to-kill orders, a sharply increasing number of refugees are fleeing political oppression and economic depression in communist-ruled Indochina.

To find the main idea in the preceding sentence, you must look at the words after the comma at the end of the opening phrase. The main idea of the sentence is "an increasing number of refugees are fleeing." The opening phrase tells us how difficult it is for them to escape.

Find the main idea in the following sentence:

> PERTH, Western Australia (Reuter)—Watched by hundreds of horrified picnickers, a 25-year-old woman burned herself to death in a Perth park Sunday by pouring petrol over her clothes and setting it alight.

Answer: A woman burned herself to death.

How to Recognize These Opening Phrases

Here are three of the most common opening phrases that do not contain the subject of the sentence.

1. A phrase that begins with a past participle.

> MONTGOMERY, Alabama (AP)—<u>Surrounded by family, dignitaries and entertainers</u>, Alabama governor George Wallace said good-bye and thank you to long-time political supporters Saturday.

MAIN IDEA: Governor George Wallace said good-bye and thank you.

> COPENHAGEN (UPI)—<u>Faced with rising inflation and a growing budget deficit</u>, 3.5 million Danes yesterday voted to choose between the Social Democrats' promise of gradual steps to economic health and the drastic measures offered by their non-socialist challengers.

MAIN IDEA: Danes voted to choose between Social Democrats and their non-socialist challengers.

> TOKYO (AP)—<u>Shaken by the US Soviet confrontation over Afghanistan</u>, Japan is gradually accepting the need for more defense spending, and is likely to give in soon to growing American pressure for a token defense buildup, a US official said yesterday.

MAIN IDEA: Japan is gradually accepting the need for more defense spending.

2. A phrase that begins with a gerund (noun consisting of a verb + ing).

> KAMPALA, Uganda (UPI)—<u>Underscoring the virtual breakdown of law and order in Uganda</u>, foreign diplomats have demanded greater military protection for both their embassies and families and indicated they might quit the troubled country if they did not receive it.

MAIN IDEA: Foreign diplomats have demanded greater protection and indicated they might quit the country (i.e., Uganda).

> LIVERPOOL, England (AP)—<u>Calling disunity among Christians a sin</u>, Pope John Paul visited Anglican and Roman Catholic cathedrals in Liverpool, the scene of Protestant-Catholic clashes for four centuries.

MAIN IDEA: Pope John Paul visited Anglican and Roman Catholic cathedrals in Liverpool.

3. A phrase that begins with a preposition. **In** is the preposition most commonly used to begin a sentence.

> HAMBURG, West Germany (UPI)—<u>In West Germany's first such case</u>, a divorced husband has sued his former wife for alimony to support him and their four children in his care.

MAIN IDEA: A divorced husband has sued his former wife.

> CAIRO, Egypt (AP)—<u>In what may be the start of Egypt's reconciliation with the Arab world</u>, Iraq recently sent a secret high-level delegation to Cairo to negotiate for Egyptian support and arms after its latest reverses in the war with Iran.

MAIN IDEA: Iraq recently sent a delegation to Cairo.

Other prepositions may also begin the lead sentence.

> MOSCOW (UPI)—<u>With the Soyuz 26 cosmonauts watching from orbit</u>, the Soyuz 27 crew undocked from the Soviet Union's space laboratory and descended to a soft landing on earth.

MAIN IDEA: The Soyuz 27 crew undocked and descended.

> MEMPHIS (Reuter)—Despite the presence of at least six potentially dangerous drugs in Elvis Presley's body, the 42-year-old king of Rock n' Roll did not die of drug abuse, the pathologist who examined Presley's remains said yesterday.

MAIN IDEA: The king of Rock n' Roll (Elvis Presley) did not die of drug abuse.

> GLASGOW, Scotland (AP)—From a hillside in Scotland, Pope John Paul II preached a sermon today of peace and reconciliation, asking the Protestants and Roman Catholics of this ancient land to make a "pilgrimage together hand in hand."

MAIN IDEA: Pope John Paul II preached a sermon today.

EXERCISE

Find the main idea in each of the following. The first one has been done for you.

1.
> TEL AVIV (UPI)—Despite *protests* by his widow, the Tel Aviv *municipal* government today knocked down the security wall around the home of the late soldier and *diplomat*, Moshe Dayan, saying it stood on public land.

MAIN IDEA: *The Tel Aviv municipal government knocked down the wall around the home of Moshe Dayan.*

2.
> TOKYO (UPI)—Apparently *succumbing* to Washington's high pressure, Japan will join the United States in clamping economic *sanctions* against Iran despite Teheran's *threat* to cut off oil supplies, government *sources* said yesterday.

MAIN IDEA:

3.
> WASHINGTON (AP)—*Ignoring protests* it was aiding "*Marxists* and *leftists*," the US Senate voted 54 to 35 Tuesday to *authorize* $75 million in *aid* to help rebuild the war-*shattered economy* of Nicaragua.

MAIN IDEA:

4.   TOKYO (Reuter)—Japan, worried about the growing *amphibious* strength of the Soviet Pacific *fleet*, plans to develop a *missile* for use against ships trying to bring *invasion* forces to the archipelago, Japanese Defense *Ministry sources* said yesterday.

MAIN IDEA:

5.   ROME (AP)—Angry because he was not given *permanent* permission to bring his small circus to *suburban* Rome, lion tamer Mario Vulcannelli took to the streets—with his eight lions.

MAIN IDEA:

6.   PHILADELPHIA (Reuter)—Declaring that Philadelphia was on the *verge* of *financial collapse, Mayor* William Green announced the *layoff* of 10 percent of the city's *workforce*, including hundreds of police officers and firemen.

MAIN IDEA:

7.   NEW YORK (AP)—Former US President Richard Nixon, considered undesirable twice by *residents* of two apartment blocks in Manhattan where he wanted to buy flats, has now bought a four-story house, the New York Times said yesterday.

MAIN IDEA:

8.   EDMONTON, Canada (AP)—An *estimated* 17,000 residents were *evacuated* from southeastern Edmonton Friday following a series of small *explosions ignited* by gas *leaking* from a *ruptured* liquefied petroleum gas pipeline.

MAIN IDEA:

9.   LONDON (AP)—Loaded with millions of dollars worth of personal gifts, Queen Elizabeth II returned Friday from a hot and socially tricky tour of seven Persian Gulf states to a wintry, strike-bound Britain.

MAIN IDEA:

10. WASHINGTON (UPI)—In an apparently *unprece-dented* move, the FBI has arranged to introduce to the news *media* a double *agent* who once *spied* on the US for the Soviets, sources said Sunday.

MAIN IDEA:

(E) Testing Your Understanding of the Lead Sentence

Quickly review the ideas presented in this chapter and then do the following exercise.

EXERCISE

Read the following newspaper leads and answer the questions. Remember to look first for the subject and main verb to help you catch the story's main idea.

1. LAKELAND, Florida (UPI)—Charlie Smith, believed to be the oldest *resident* of the United States at age 137, was *hospitalized* Wednesday complaining of shortness of breath but was reported in fair condition and resting comfortably.

According to the story, where is Charlie Smith now?
What do people believe about him?
The story said he was having trouble _____ ing.

2. LAKEPORT, Michigan (AP)—A missing guard was arrested yesterday in the *theft* of more than 1.5 million dollars in cash he was assigned to protect, state police said.

What was the guard's job?
What did he do instead?
Was the guard found?
What happened to him?

3. WASHINGTON (AP)—The life expectancy of Asian children has increased sharply over the past two *decades* and a child born in Asia in 1975 could expect to live an average of 56 years—almost 10 years longer than those born in 1960, the World Bank said in a report *issued* yesterday.

How long could a child born in Asia in 1960 expect to live?
Can an Asian child born today expect to live longer?

4.   CHICAGO (AP)—*Researchers* say they have learned how to grow human cancer *tumors* in the *laboratory*, a *feat* that may eventually enable doctors to predict what cancer-fighting drugs will be effective with which patients.

What do researchers say they have learned to do?
Why is this important?

5.   BELGRADE (AP)—Edvard Kardelj, Yugoslavia's No. 2 *political figure* and President Tito's closest *aide* for more than 40 years, died yesterday in a Ljubljana hospital at the age of 69, doctors announced.

How many people died in this story?

6.   UNITED NATIONS (AP)—Over American and Soviet *protest*, the first billion-dollar *budget* in the 33-year history of the United Nations was recommended Friday by the *General Assembly's* Budgetary Committee, made up of all UN members.

What is the main idea of this story?
Were earlier UN budgets more or less than one billion dollars?
Are the United States and the Soviet Union members of the
    committee that recommends the budget?
Did these two countries support the new budget?

7.   RANGOON, Burma (UPI)—Two Burmese doctors believe throat *cancer* among Burmese may be caused by the chewing of betel and cigar smoking, habits common among the country's *peasants*.

What may be the cause of throat cancer among the Burmese?
If this is true, which group of people would you expect to get this
    disease often?
Give reasons for your answer to the preceding question.

8.   COPENHAGEN, Denmark (UPI)—Greenland, the world's largest island, has *voted* in favor of home rule for its 50,000 *inhabitants*, ending more than 250 years of Danish *colonial status*, nearly complete *returns* showed yesterday.

Did the people of Greenland vote for independence or to remain a
    colony?
Have all the votes been counted?
How many people live in Greenland?

9. ROME (AP)—*Striking* in early morning *raids* in fashionable neighborhoods throughout Italy today, police *squads arrested* 38 bank presidents and other *prominent* businessmen yesterday and charged them with participating in a nationwide *scandal.*

What happened in this story and why?

10. SINGAPORE (AP)—A *legal battle* over a dead man's multi-million dollar *fortune* involving *rival claims* by his family and Indonesia's state-owned Pertamina Oil company begins in the Singapore high *court* on March 10.

What is the main idea of the story? (Be brief.)
Who is involved in the "legal battle"?
What do they want?

11. SAN FRANCISCO, California (AP)—Like Santa Clauses in reverse, *thieves* slipped through a skylight in the roof of a museum here and made off with a million-dollar Rembrandt and three other Dutch Renaissance paintings.

Is this a story about Santa Claus?
Who is the story about?
What did they do?
How many paintings are mentioned in the story?
Who was Rembrandt?

12. BELGRADE (AP)—Despite efforts by Yugoslav *officials* to *ignore* reports that 86-year-old President Josip Broz Tito has *divorced* his second wife and married a 35-year-old opera singer, *rumors* of a new marriage persist.

Has President Tito divorced his second wife and married a 35-year-old opera singer?

13. SYDNEY, Australia (UPI)—The father of a light aircraft pilot who disappeared mysteriously over Bass Strait in October after reportedly sighting an *unidentified* object has *appealed* to oceanographer Jacques Cousteau for help in searching for his son.

Who disappeared in the story?
Where and when did he disappear?
Who has asked for help?
Who has been asked to help?

14. BEIRUT (UPI)—Five Lebanese Muslim *hijackers armed* with guns and hand *grenades released* 73 passengers and nine *crew* members of a Middle East Airlines jet yesterday after a six-and-a-half hour air *piracy* drama.

Did the hijackers hurt the passengers and crew members?
What weapons did the hijackers have?
How long did they keep the passengers in the plane?
Find an expression in this lead that means **hijacking an airplane**.

(F) *A Final Note About Leads*

This chapter has discussed the most common English language newspaper lead—the summary lead. Its purpose is to give you the story's main topic and its most important facts. If you read a newspaper, however, you will soon discover some stories that use another type of lead. Here is an example:

LONDON (AP)—Too old, too ill, too fond of food and drink, too vain to wear their spectacles, sometimes overdrugged.

This is clearly not a summary lead because it does not even tell you the story's subject. It is not until the second paragraph that you learn that this story is about a British doctor's opinion of past and present world leaders.

The purpose of such a lead is simply to catch your interest, trying to make you read further. You will study stories that use such leads in chapter 7, Other Kinds of Newspaper Writing. To understand **interest catchers**, therefore, you must do just that: continue reading.

Beyond the Lead

In this chapter you will learn how to read the rest of the news story. You will learn to anticipate what the story contains and to recognize and understand words and phrases that refer to information mentioned earlier in the story.

(A) How to Anticipate What a Story Contains

It is often possible to guess much of what a story will talk about just by reading the lead. Let's take an example:

> GATLINBURG, Tennessee (AP)—A pilot whose plane crashed in a cushion of snow atop a 5,500-foot peak survived 16 hours in sub-zero weather by stuffing newspapers and air charts into his clothing to keep warm, rescuers said.

This, like most good leads, has given you the topic and main facts of the story.

TOPIC: A pilot survived a plane crash.
MAIN FACTS:

1. The plane crashed on a snow-covered mountain top.
2. The pilot was not killed.
3. The weather was very cold.
4. The pilot survived for 16 hours.
5. He put newspapers and air charts into his clothing to keep warm.
6. He was rescued.
7. Associated Press got the story on Tuesday from the rescuers.

This is a lot of information, but it is not the whole story. There are still unanswered questions. Was the pilot badly hurt in the crash? Who rescued him and how? Where is the mountain? Where was the pilot going and where had he come from? Was he alone? You can expect these questions to be answered in the rest of the story!

Good journalists know the questions their readers will ask and answer them. Finish the story and see if our questions were actually answered.

Paragraph	Questions answered or new information introduced	Story
2	Where was the mountain? When was the pilot found? What was his name? How old was he? What condition was he in?	When rescuers reached him in the ice-covered Great National Park after day-break, Bill Bruning, 32, of Jonesboro, Georgia, was in good condition.
3	Could he walk? Who rescued him? How was he rescued?	"It feels good to walk, I've been wrapped up all night," he said, spurning offers from park rangers to carry him 500 yards to an evacuation helicopter.
4	How did he feel? What was the weather like?	"I feel fine. It was pretty cold out there but it was a short night."
5	How badly was he hurt? How did the cold weather affect him?	Dr. Robert Lash, a Federal Aviation Administration medical examiner, said Bruning had several facial cuts, bruises on his back, a mildly frost-bitten right foot and was suffering slightly from hypothermia, a lowering of the body temperature.
6	What happened during the night? Did the pilot sleep?	Officials kept in radio contact with Bruning through the night and, afraid he might freeze to death, allowed him to sleep only 45 minutes.
7	What kind of a plane was it? Where was the pilot coming from? Where was he going? Where did the plane crash? Was anyone with the pilot?	Bruning's single-engine Piper tripacer was bound from Atlanta to Knoxville's Airport when it crashed near Siler's Bald—just on the North Carolina side of the mountain and about 100 yards from the Appalachian trail. He was alone.

So the story did answer our questions. It even answered questions we hadn't thought to ask.

A good reader asks questions. A good reader wants to know more facts than those given in the lead. Such questions are useful because they give your reading a purpose. It is much easier to understand a story when you are actively looking for information.

EXERCISE

Read the following leads and decide what questions you think the writer will answer in the rest of the story. You will find the complete stories in the answer key so you can check to see if the questions were actually answered.

Some of your questions will probably be about vocabulary. In number one, for example, you might ask: "What is a respirator?" This is a very useful kind of question and it is one that you can often answer just by reading the story.

1.

> LOS ANGELES (Reuter)—While his parents sat by his side, a three-year-old boy died here Friday night just 17 minutes after doctors switched off his life-saving respirator.

Which of the following questions do you expect the rest of the story to answer?
   a. Why did the doctors switch off the respirator?
   b. What is a respirator?
   c. Why was the boy in the hospital?
   d. How much did it cost to stay in the hospital?
   e. Is a respirator expensive?
   f. Did the parents want the doctors to switch off the respirator?
   g. Was it against the law to let the boy die?
   h. Was it a government hospital or a private hospital?

2.

> LONDON (UPI)—Hairdresser Carl Moss, depressed by money problems and a break with his girlfriend tried to commit suicide six times in one night, and failed, police told a court of Chichester, 71 miles southwest of London yesterday.

Which of the following questions do you expect the rest of the story to answer?
   a. How long had Carl Moss been a hairdresser?
   b. What was the name of his girlfriend?
   c. What kind of money problems did he have?
   d. What does it mean to commit suicide?
   e. How did Carl Moss try to commit suicide?
   f. Why did he fail?
   g. How many people were in the court?
   h. What happened to Carl Moss?

3.

> CHICAGO (Reuter)—A pilot pulled an American Airlines Boeing 727 sharply out of a landing approach as he saw another airliner taking off across his path yesterday at Chicago's O'Hare Airport, officials said.

Use the following key words to make questions about the story. Then check the answer key.

a. How close?   d. Name—other airliner?
b. Why—happen?   e. How many passengers?
c. Weather?   f. Who—officials?

Now read the following three stories and decide what questions you would want answered. Check the answer key to see if your questions were indeed answered.

4. | SAN QUENTIN, California (Reuter)—Three men in a tub named "Rub-a-Dub-Dub" escaped from San Quentin prison after rejecting an offer of help from an unsuspecting guard.

5. | LONDON (AP)—Cooks and other catering staff on Britain's North Sea oil rigs have gone on strike for more pay.

6. | MYRTLE BEACH, South Carolina (AP)—A blonde, blue-eyed 5-year-old girl leaped joyfully into the arms of her parents late Monday, just hours after a high-speed car chase ended with her rescue from an alleged abductor.

(B) *Recognizing Information Introduced Earlier in the Story*

It is important that you learn to recognize the parts of the story that refer to information introduced earlier.

The most common references are:
- Pronouns and Possessive Adjectives

WASHINGTON (UPI)—President Carter signed the $227.7 billion oil-windfall profits tax Wednesday, just short of a year after he sent it to Congress.

he = President Carter
it = oil-windfall profits tax

> COLUMBUS, Ohio (UPI)—Surgeons at Ohio State University are turning a technique developed by the Russians into a weight-control measure for grossly fat people—<u>they</u> are stapling <u>their</u> stomachs shut.

they = Surgeons
their = grossly fat people

- The Definite Article: **The**

> ATEOS, El Salvador (AP)—An earthquake rocked El Salvador early Saturday, hurling huge boulders onto highways, causing landslides and toppling rural houses. Officials said 12 persons were killed and more than 220 injured.
> <u>The quake</u>, centered in the Pacific Ocean about 60 miles south of San Salvador, the capital, also was felt strongly in Guatemala, Nicaragua and Honduras.

The quake = An earthquake

> MEXICO CITY (UPI)—Cuba has freed 400 political prisoners, bringing the number of those released this year to 3,200, Cuba's official news agency Prensa Latina reported.
> In a Havana-datelined dispatch Monday, <u>the agency</u> said <u>the 400</u> formed the seventh group of prisoners released because of dialog between Fidel Castro's Government and Cuban exiles begun last December.

the agency = Cuba's official news agency Prensa Latina
the 400 = 400 political prisoners

EXERCISE

Read the following and answer the questions.

> 1.   DAMASCUS, Syria (AP)—Thousands of Syrians, Palestinians and Lebanese *refugees demonstrated* today outside the US *Embassy* against the Israeli *invasion* of Lebanon and what <u>they</u> called American *complicity* in <u>it</u>.
> From early morning, <u>the demonstrators</u> surged through the streets shouting *slogans* and carrying *banners condemning* the invasion and calling for the downfall of the US government.

What does **they** refer to?
What does **it** refer to?
Who are **the demonstrators**?

2.
> NAGASAKI, Japan (Reuter)—*Surgeons* have stitched back in place a hand and the whole forearm of a 17-year-old mechanic after they were severed in a motor winch accident, doctors said here yesterday.

What does the pronoun **they** refer to in this story?

3.
> BRIDGEPORT, Connecticut (UPI)—A Vietnamese woman seeking *custody* of two sons she left with an adoption agency in Saigon during the final days of the Vietnam War will be able to visit the boys next week.

Who are **the boys** mentioned in the story?

4.
> JAKARTA (AFP)—Police in Jakarta have uncovered an all-woman *pickpocket gang* led by "a wife of a government official" and *arrested* six of them, it was reported here yesterday.
>
> The large circulation Jakarta daily "Kompas" said the detained women were all married, had their own homes and ranged in age from 25 to 45.

Who does the expression **six of them** refer to?
Who are **the detained women**?

5.
> AGANA, Guam (Reuter)—Governor Ricardo Bord-Allo declared a state of *emergency* on Guam yesterday as a *gigantic* typhoon, packing winds gusting to 195 miles (310 kilometers) an hour, bore down on this tiny American trust territory.
>
> US Navy *authorities* declared the 30-mile-long Pacific paradise island in typhoon Condition One at mid-afternoon yesterday, meaning the twisting storm was expected to hit within 12 hours.

What does **this tiny American trust territory** refer to?
What does **the 30-mile-long Pacific paradise island** refer to?
What does the story mean by **the twisting storm**?

6.
> GENEVA (Reuter)—The United Nations Tuesday decided to open a bank account to help poor countries offer new homes to the small-scale farmers, fishermen and craft workers who make up most of the world's 10 million *refugees*.
>
> The decision to set up the *voluntary* fund followed a report by the UN High Commissioner for Refugees that industrialized countries had taken in hundreds of *refugees* from *urban* backgrounds, but found it difficult to absorb *rural* workers.

Specifically, what is **the decision** mentioned in paragraph two?

7. WASHINGTON (AP)—Federal safety officials *urged* 35 states Friday to raise their drinking age to 21, noting that a third of the people killed in alcohol-related accidents are between the ages of 16 and 24.

"This is a national *tragedy* and a national *scandal*," said James Burnett, chairman of the National Transportation Safety Board, which called for a minimum drinking age of 21 nationwide.

What does **this** in paragraph two refer to?

8. MANILA (Reuter)—Plunging necklines, see-through dresses and rising skirt slits are causing *turmoil* at the Philippine National Labor Relations Commission.

Alarmed at the way its female employees adapted their *uniforms* to emphasize sex appeal and fearing that the work of young males was suffering, the *Commission* set up a committee to examine the problem, officials said yesterday.

The Committee *decreed*: "No strapless or spaghetti-strapped dresses, no see-through dresses with plunging necklines and definitely no thigh-hugging or high-slit skirts."

But the order ran into immediate trouble with *rank and file employees* defending their right to be entertained at work and the more daring girls *challenging* their bosses to send them home if they thought their uniforms went too far.

Now the order has been *suspended* and the Committee which made it has *resigned*, Miss Lowaywa Ylegan, its secretary and the assistant personnel officer, told Reuter.

Whose female employees does the story talk about?
What is the commission mentioned in paragraph two?
What is the problem mentioned in paragraph two?
What is the order mentioned in paragraph four?
What do the underlined words in paragraph four refer to?
their:
them:
they:

(C) *How to Read the Typical News Story*

In most news stories the most important facts will be found near the beginning—usually within the first two or three paragraphs. The remainder of the story will give details explaining and clarifying the main points, or introducing new, but less important information.

Here is a formula for a typical news story.

Paragraph One	• The story's subject and most important facts
Paragraph Two	• Important facts that the writer was unable to include in the lead
	• Information to clarify the facts in the lead
	• A particularly important quote
The rest of the story	• Specific details to answer readers' questions
	• Statements and opinions by people involved in the story or by outside observers
	• Background information
	• New, but less important facts

There is a good reason why the most important information comes near the beginning. Newspapers have limited space and stories are often edited (cut). In fact, the lead is sometimes the only part of the story that gets into the newspaper.

If you know how a news story is written, you also know how to read it.

1. Read the beginning of the story very carefully because it contains the most important facts.
2. Try to anticipate what will follow in the rest of the story. If you find yourself reading about a murder, for example, you can expect to find the answers to questions such as:
   • Who was murdered?
   • Who was the murderer?
   • How was the victim murdered?
   • What was the reason for the murder?
   • Has the murderer been caught?
3. If you don't understand something at the beginning of a story, keep reading. You will often get a second (and perhaps a third) chance to understand.

EXERCISE

It is very important to realize that you often get two or three chances to understand the story's main points. In the following exercise, read the opening paragraph of each story and note the main points. Then read the rest of the story and find where the main points are explained in greater detail.

1. GENEVA (AP)—A prisoner threw herself from the sixth story roof of a jail during a prison *revolt* here last night.

Swiss *authorities* said the woman, who apparently fell into a safety net, was taken to hospital but was not seriously *injured*.

MAIN POINTS
- There was a prisoner's revolt.
- A prisoner threw herself off the jail roof.
- She was not seriously injured.

Now read the rest of the story and answer the following:
a. The story names the jail in paragraph(s) _____ .
b. The story describes the jail in paragraph(s) _____ .
c. The story explains the reason for the prison revolt in paragraph(s) _____ .
d. The story explains why the woman jumped in paragraph(s) _____ .
e. The story describes the revolt in paragraph(s) _____ .
f. The story introduces additional background information in paragraph(s) _____ .

PARAGRAPH

3   She leaped from the roof of the Champ Dollon Modele jail when guards turned fire hoses on 60 men and women prisoners *demonstrating* on the roof for improved conditions of detention.

4   Other inmates in the mixed prison, the most modern in Switzerland, set up a *racket* in their *cells* which could be heard some distance away.

5   The demonstration ended soon after the woman's fall from the roof. Police *declined* to *reveal* her identity.

6   West German *terrorist* Gabriele Kroecher-Tiedemmann is one of the jail's 200 inmates, *serving a* 14-year *sentence* for *wounding* two *customs officers* at the Swiss-French *border*.

7   Police said she played no part in the revolt, being in the jail's top *security* wing out of touch with her fellow inmates.

2. MOSCOW (UPI)—Moscow recorded its coldest year-end weather in 100 years yesterday and the *weather bureau predicted* an all-time record low for winter was just around the corner.

MAIN POINTS
- Moscow had its coldest year-end weather in 100 years yesterday.
- The weather bureau predicted an all-time record soon.

Now read the rest of the story and answer the following:
  a. The story tells how cold it was yesterday in paragraph(s) _____ .

  b. The story tells the coldest year-end temperature in paragraph(s) _____ .

  c. The story tells when the all-time coldest temperature was recorded in paragraph(s) _____ .

  d. The story tells how cold it is expected to get and when this will happen in paragraph(s) _____ .

PARAGRAPH

2   The Moscow regional weather bureau said temperatures fell to minus 33° F early yesterday— two degrees colder than the mark set in 1915. It was the coldest December 30 since the bureau began keeping records 100 years ago.

3   The weather bureau forecast overnight temperatures today as low as minus 49° F. The record low for a Moscow winter is minus 44° F.

3. | CHICAGO (Reuter)—Chicago's 48,600 teachers and other employees are without pay over Christmas because of a *financial crisis* in the city's public school system, second largest in the United States.

MAIN POINTS
  • Chicago's teachers and other school employees will not be paid because of a financial crisis.

Now read the rest of the story and answer the following:
  a. The story explains what the crisis is in paragraph(s)_____ .
  b. The story explains the cause of the crisis in paragraph(s) _____ .

  c. The story describes possible solutions to the crisis in paragraph(s) _____ .

  d. The story gives the reaction of the teachers and employees in paragraph(s) _____ .

  e. The story tells when the teachers and employees will be paid in paragraph(s) _____ .

PARAGRAPH

2   The Chicago Board of Education had only $8.7 million in the bank Friday to meet its fortnightly *payroll* of $41.5 million.

3   It had been counting on a last-minute bailout from Illinois Governor Jim Thompson with a $50 million state loan that did not materialize.

4   The 26,000-strong Teachers *Union* said that unless its members were paid they would not report for work when schools reopen on January 2 after a Christmas break.

5   The board's president, Mrs. William Rohter, said the employees would be paid as soon as a *rescue* plan had been worked out with city and state officials. She said she hoped normal classes would *resume* on January 2.

6   A committee *appointed* by Chicago Mayor Jayne Byrne to look into the *finances* of the city's 640 elementary and high schools reported that they would need $694 million to keep going until August.

7   It said the board would have to close some schools *temporarily* and *drastically slash* its *budget* unless the school system received a big injection of *capital*.

Now go back and review the method for reading a typical news story on page 40. Then use the method with one or two of the example stories in the back of this book, or with news stories in an English language newspaper. Don't worry too much about vocabulary at this point. That is the subject for the next chapter.

(D) *Background and Interpretation*

Some of the people who read newspapers are very well informed. They are familiar with the major stories of the day and have a good understanding of the world situation. Many other people, however, are not so well informed. In fact, they may know very little about what is happening in the world. The news writer must write for both types of people. When reporting a story, the news writer must provide key facts for the well informed and must also include background and interpretation for those who may be unfamiliar with the subject matter. The following example illustrates how this idea works. The following news report concerns the launching of a rocket. This is not an unusual occurrence in our modern world, but note how the writer provides background information to explain why this particular launch is a significant one.

PARIS, France (AP)—Scientists in French Guiana began the daylong countdown Wednesday for the most crucial launch in the history of the problem-plagued European space program.

Today's scheduled liftoff will be the sixth test for the three-stage Ariane rocket, which has failed twice. A third failure could sink the program as deep as Ariane 5, which plunged into the South Atlantic in September after a fuel pump malfunctioned.

Industry officials say a third failure would cause many clients to use the escape clause in their contracts; several firms, including Western Union, have already booked backup reservations on the competing U.S. space shuttle.

Let's continue with this same story and see how it was reported **the next day**. Note that the writer does not assume that the reader is familiar with the story. He still provides almost the same background as he did the previous day.

> KOUROU, French Guiana (AP)—The European launcher Ariane 6 sent two communications satellites into orbit Thursday, giving a crucial boost to Europe's space program and its chances of breaking the superpowers' monopoly on space.
>
> It was the European Space Agency's sixth attempt to get the three-stage Ariane rocket off the ground. Two launches ended in failure. A third setback could have wrecked the program. Ariane 5 crashed into the sea with $50 million worth of satellites last September after a fuel pump failed.

Background and interpretation make the story more meaningful to the reader. Such information should be especially useful to you as a beginning newspaper reader.

Some common uses of background and interpretation include:

1. IDENTIFICATION

> Sirhan Sirhan, convicted killer of Sen. Robert F. Kennedy, told parole board members that he had no reason to expect them to be fair to him.

2. INTERPRETATION

> As a result of Sunday's election, the size of the lower house in the Bundestag was increased from 496 members to 498. It is not unusual for the chamber's size to change this way in the course of an election.

3. EXPLANATION

> The West German voting system is one of Europe's most complicated. Each voter casts two ballots, one for the district representative and the other for a political party.

Note that the writer can include background or interpretation in three ways: (1) as part of a sentence, (2) as a complete sentence at the end of a paragraph, or (3) as a complete paragraph.

EXERCISE

Read the following stories and answer the questions.

1.   COLOGNE, West Germany (AP)—Rain-swollen rivers isolated towns, knocked out power and ravaged crops Sunday in West Germany's worst flooding in 36 years.

Hundreds of homes and shops were *inundated* in the second major flood in barely six weeks and the third this year. Damage was still being assessed but was estimated in the millions of dollars.

a. How does this flood compare to previous floods?
b. Does flooding appear to be unusual in this part of Germany?

2.   NEW YORK (AP)—Isidore Zimmerman, who spent 24 years in prison and came within two hours of dying in the electric chair for a murder he didn't commit, was awarded $1 million in damages from the state of New York Tuesday.

State Court of Claims Judge Joseph Modugno ruled that the award was "fair and reasonable" *compensation* for "loss of earnings, medical expenses, loss of liberty and civil rights, loss of reputation and mental anguish."

The award was the largest for wrongful imprisonment anyone could recall in New York State, and one of the largest in U.S. history. It was granted because the state's Court of Claims last November accepted Zimmerman's argument that he was convicted because of *prosecutorial* misconduct.

Zimmerman was 21 in 1938 when he was convicted of murder and sentenced to death for allegedly supplying a gun used in a Lower East Side restaurant holdup in which a New York City detective was killed.

On Jan. 6, 1939, two hours before his scheduled execution, Gov. Herbert Lehman commuted the death sentence to life imprisonment. Zimmerman—who had always insisted he was innocent of the crime—sought *vindication* for years through the state's courts and Legislature.

In 1961, Zimmerman was released after the state Court of Appeals threw out his murder conviction on grounds of prosecutorial misconduct. Zimmerman had by then spent 24 years in maximum security prisons in which he had often been held in *solitary confinement*.

Zimmerman *sued* for $10 million.

a. What happened in this story? (1 sentence)
b. Briefly (4 sentences) give the background to this court decision.
c. How does the money awarded in this case compare with previous cases of this type?

3.

WASHINGTON (UPI)—The carrier USS Coral Sea was to enter the Mediterranean Wednesday, at least temporarily increasing U.S. naval air power within reach of the Middle East.

Defense and navy officials denied reports that the appearance of the Coral Sea in the Mediterranean is intended to signal the Soviets and the Syrians to back off from any possible military moves in the continuing Lebanon crisis.

The carrier, accompanied by a *frigate*, a guided-missile destroyer and a refueling tanker, passed through the Suez Canal after a voyage from the Pacific across the Indian Ocean, officials said.

According to the latest reports, U.S. and Soviet naval strength is close to normal levels in the Mediterranean despite persistent tensions in the Lebanon area, where Israeli forces confront the Syrians.

a. What is the significance of the movement of the carrier USS Coral Sea?
b. What reasons did some reports give for this movement?
c. How did the U.S. military react to these reports?
d. Has there been a major buildup of U.S. and Soviet naval forces in the Mediterranean?

Understanding Words in Context

In this chapter you will learn how to decide when and when not to use your dictionary. You will also learn several methods for guessing the meanings of new words.

New vocabulary is usually the biggest problem for people learning to read an English language newspaper. Each story contains many unknown words and learners quickly tire of having to use their dictionaries so often. Actually, a dictionary is less necessary than many people think. Here are some suggestions for you to use before you look a word up.

(A) When Not to Use the Dictionary

Going to the dictionary too often wastes time and may actually hurt your understanding of the story. You should instead be looking for the story's main ideas. You can do this without understanding every word. A good rule for the beginning reader might be:

> Never use your dictionary until you are sure it is necessary.

First ask yourself these questions:

1. Can I understand the sentence without understanding the new word?
2. Do I need to understand the exact meaning of the word, or is it enough to have a general idea of its meaning?

The meaning of a sentence is often clear without understanding all the words. Look at the following example:

> MIAMI (Reuter)—The first contingent of Cuban political prisoners to be reunited with their friends and families in the United States arrived here Saturday.

If you are a beginning reader, you probably don't know the word **contingent**. But you can understand the sentence without it. The main idea is quite clear: "Cuban political prisoners . . . arrived here (in Miami) Saturday."

Sometimes the exact meaning of a word is not necessary. It is enough to see that the word refers to a person, a place, a piece of equipment, a movement, something good or something bad, etc. Take, for example, the word **flocked** in the following.

> NICOSIA (UPI)—Thousands of Greek Cypriots flocked to Kykko monastery today to pay homage to Archibishop Makarios on the first anniversary of his death.

Flocked refers to:
   a. a sound   b. a path   c. a movement   d. a place

The correct answer is, of course, a movement. The exact meaning is unnecessary. The important thing is that we know that the people went in some way to Kykko monastery.

EXERCISE

Read the following lead sentences and decide which of these three choices best fits each underlined word.

   A. The story can be understood without this word.
   B. It is possible to get a general idea of the word's meaning from the story and this is enough.
   C. The exact meaning of the word is important to the understanding of the story. Unless the meaning becomes clear from the rest of the story, it will be necessary to look it up in the dictionary.

Note that the last choice (C) did not say that you must immediately look the word up. Always continue reading first because new words often become clear in later parts of the story.

1.
> NAPLES, Italy (UPI)—Beleaguered Italian doctors sought the help of US and European experts yesterday to combat the mysterious "dark disease" that has killed 60 infants in the Naples area over the past year.

beleaguered _____   combat _____

2.   SALINAS, California (AP)—A prisoner with both hands and feet <u>fettered</u>, escaped by jumping from a plane as it landed at Salinas Airport on Thursday, police reported here yesterday.

fettered _____

3.   CALCUTTA (Reuter)—Seventy-four people were drowned near Calcutta when their bus <u>skidded</u> off the road into deep waters, an official spokesman said here yesterday.

skidded _____

4.   KNOXVILLE, Iowa (UPI)—<u>Scoffing</u> at President Carter's grain <u>embargo</u>, Senator Edward Kennedy yesterday said it would have only one effect: "The Russians are going to eat a little more chicken and a little less meat."

scoffing _____   embargo _____

5.   THE HAGUE (Reuter)—Queen Juliana of the Netherlands may <u>abdicate</u> in favor of her eldest daughter, former Princess Beatrix, informed sources said.

abdicate _____

6.   COLOMBO (AFP)—A new local liquor <u>tavern</u> was ordered closed by the Government Wednesday hardly eight hours after it opened following a protest by Buddhist monks.

tavern _____

7.   FLINTSTONE, Md. (AP)—The Allegany County Health Department says a <u>raccoon</u> found in the Flintstone area was confirmed as having <u>rabies</u>.

raccoon _____   rabies _____

8.   JAKARTA (UPI)—Police yesterday <u>clamped</u> a dusk to dawn curfew on the capital city of Ujungpandang in south Sulawesi following two days of rioting and looting of shops by thousands of youths.

clamped _____

9. | KABUL (UPI)—The US Embassy in the Afghan capital is cutting back its already <u>drastically</u> reduced staff because of uncertainty over the military situation, Western diplomatic sources said yesterday.

drastically _____

10. | PANAMA CITY (AP)—The Panamanian Government has offered to give political <u>asylum</u> to the leftist guerrillas holding dozens of foreign diplomats in the embassy of the Dominican Republic in Bogota, Colombia, a top Panamanian diplomat said today.

asylum _____

(B) Guessing a Word's Meaning

It is often possible to get a clear understanding of a word just from reading the sentence where you find it.

| SKEGNESS, England (Reuter)—Two pet Alsatian dogs savaged a six-year-old girl to death here yesterday, police said.

If you picture in your mind how a dog kills a person, you have the exact meaning of **savaged** in the sentence. Try the same idea with the following exercise.

EXERCISE

Read each sentence and try to figure out the meanings of the underlined words without using a dictionary.

1. | TEL AVIV (AP)—Iraq and Syria have reportedly agreed to <u>merge</u> under a single leader and combine their armies on Israel's northeastern border, Israel said Sunday.

merge: a. attack   b. disagree   c. join   d. discuss

2. | HANNOVER, West Germany (UPI)—An East German couple, flying low to <u>evade</u> radar controls, escaped to the West Thursday in a crop-dusting aircraft, police reported.

evade: a. use   b. find   c. avoid   d. try

3. BEDFORD, Massachusetts (UPI)—Three men attempting to be the first to reach Europe by balloon passed Newfoundland, <u>drifted</u> out over the North Atlantic and reported "everything's going just fine."

drift: a. float in the wind   c. move on wheels
        b. be pulled by a vehicle   d. fall

4. SAN SALVADOR, El Salvador (AP)—The family of Israel's Honorary Consul <u>pleaded</u> Thursday for his release by unknown kidnappers because he is in poor health and needs medicine.

plead: a. make a strong threat
        b. make a funny statement
        c. make a statement of support
        d. make a deeply felt request

5. MANILA (UPI)—the Philippines will issue an <u>ultimatum</u> today to the Vietnamese refugee boat Tung An to leave for Hong Kong or be <u>towed</u> forcibly to international waters, well-informed sources said yesterday.

ultimatum: a. polite request   c. formal invitation
            b. final order   d. announcement of help
tow: a. pull   b. help   c. guide   d. shoot

51

6.

> NEW YORK (Reuter)—New York's buses and under-
> ground trains were rolling again yesterday after an 11-
> day strike that caused traffic <u>chaos</u> and cost the city an
> estimated $1.11 billion in lost revenue and production.

chaos: a. control   c. manners
           b. confusion   d. methods

7.

> NEW YORK (UPI)—Marathon swimmer George
> Kauffman had planned to swim around the island of
> Manhattan twice, but after completing the first <u>circuit</u>
> he decided once was enough.

circuit: a. path of electrical current   c. part
          b. time around   d. plan

(C) Looking for Explanations

A news writer knows that many readers have had very little
education, or they lack the background to understand the technical
terms that are occasionally found in news stories. The writer
therefore explains anything that a large number of readers might
not understand. Learn to look for these explanations and you will
avoid wasting time with your dictionary.

Sometimes the writer merely adds an explanatory phrase to a
sentence. Such a phrase follows immediately after the word to be
explained. We have already seen an example of this in the story
about the pilot who survived a plane crash.

> **Bruning was suffering slightly from hypothermia, a
> lowering of the body temperature.**

Few readers would know what "hypothermia" meant without
the writer's explanatory note: a lowering of the body temperature.

If the explanation is more difficult, the writer may add a full
sentence or even two.

> The earthquake measured 6.5 on the Richter scale. <u>The
> Richter scale measures the magnitude of the earth-
> quake in graded steps from 1 to 10, with each step
> approximately 60 times greater than the preceding
> step.</u>

EXERCISE

Read the following stories and look for explanations to clarify
the underlined words.

1.

> ST. LOUIS (AP)—A brasher <u>doubloon</u>, one of the
> first gold coins minted in the United States, was sold
> Friday for an apparent world record price of $430,000.

2.   NEW DEHLI (Reuter)—An encephalitis outbreak has claimed 325 lives in the past month, a State Health Department spokesman said yesterday.

        Encephalitis, a viral brain disease spread by mosquitoes, killed 2,715 people in India last year, according to official statistics.

3.   WASHINGTON (UPI)—The Federal Aviation Administration concluded yesterday that the DC-10 pylon, the structure that attaches the engine to the wing, is fundamentally sound and does not need any major design changes.

4.   DURHAM, North Carolina (AP)—New fossil evidence indicates a small ape-like creature which lived 30 million years ago is the oldest known common ancestor of man and apes, a Duke University anthropologist said Wednesday.

        Dr. Elwyn L. Simons, head of Duke's Center for the Study of Primate Biology and History, said at a news conference that he and his colleagues have determined that the animal lived in a complex social group defended by large males.

        The creature is known as Aegyptopithecus Zeoxis, which means "connecting ape of Egypt," Simons said.

5.   TOKYO (UPI)—A group of Japanese scientists said Saturday hydrogen peroxide, a food additive widely used for pastry, has been found to be cancer-causing.

        Prof. Akiniro Itoh of Hiroshima University who led the research on the substance said his report was based on experiments with mice. He added, however, it was not immediately known whether the additive would be harmful to human beings.

        Hydrogen peroxide is widely used as a bleach or sterilizer for pastry and a variety of fish pastes.

D) *Using the Second Chance*

Because the main points in the lead are usually repeated and explained later in the story, you really get two chances to understand them. The same is true of vocabulary. Therefore, if you don't understand a word, keep reading. You may find that the writer uses the same idea again but in a word or phrase that you do understand.

Look for Synonyms!

Two words are synonyms if they have the same or nearly the same meanings. Whenever possible, writers of English use synonyms to avoid repeating the same word and boring their readers.

Learn to look for these synonyms and you will find yourself using your dictionary less and less often.

Find a synonym for the word **fatigue** in the following.

> JERUSALEM (Reuter)—Prime Minister Menachem Begin was under care in hospital yesterday after complaining of <u>fatigue.</u>
>
> The 65-year-old Israeli leader was rushed in for treatment Friday night. His spokesman, Don Patio, said the Prime Minister had been overcome by tiredness, but was expected out of hospital by tonight.

The synonym is, of course, **tiredness**. So even if you didn't know the word **fatigue**, you still didn't need a dictionary to find out what it meant.

The definite article (**the**) before a word or phrase is also a good signal that you may have found a synonym for a previously mentioned idea.

Find a synonym for the word **reassessment** in the following.

> CANBERRA (Reuter)—Australian worries over events in Kampuchea and other trouble spots have caused the government to order a full-scale <u>reassessment</u> of Australia's defense position, officials said.
>
> Prime Minister Malcom Fraser said in a television interview that the review would take months to complete. He pointed to developments in Indochina, Iran, and Korea as reasons for the study.

Actually there are two synonyms, **review** and **study**. Note also that the second paragraph explains the **trouble spots** mentioned in paragraph one. Can you find out what they are?

EXERCISE

Read the following and answer the questions.

1.
> KOCHI, Japan (UPI)—A 22-year-old housewife using a fertility drug yesterday gave birth to <u>quadruplets</u> at the Kochi Municipal Hospital in this southwestern Japanese city, a hospital report said.
>
> The four babies, three boys and one girl, were born underweight, but are in satisfactory condition in incubators. The mother, Mrs. Kazuki Takeda, was also in good condition, the report said.

The **quadruplets** in this story are:
- a. fertility drugs
- b. four babies
- c. incubators
- d. hospital reports

54

2. QUEBEC (UPI)—An unidentified gunman who held 12 <u>hostages</u> in a suburban bank branch for more than nine hours, escaped with the bank manager and a woman as prisoners late Monday night after the other hostages were released.

The **hostages** in this story are:
  a. gunmen   c. bank managers
  b. bank branches   d. prisoners

3. NEW YORK (UPI)—Detectives, <u>posing</u> as foreign tourists who couldn't speak English, arrested two taxi drivers at Kennedy Airport Friday for allegedly charging up to $60 for a trip that normally costs $3.

    District Attorney John Santucci said the officers were told to pretend to be tourists and mingle with the crowd with money in one hand and a slip of paper with the address of the hotel in the other.

A synonym for **pose** in this story is:
  a. charge   b. arrest   c. pretend   d. mingle

4. BROADUS, Montana (AP)—A fly flew through an open window and into the mouth of truck driver Arthur Tiffit of Spokane, Washington, causing him to begin choking and to lose control of his <u>rig</u>, officials said.

The **rig** in this story is:
  a. a fly   b. a person   c. a truck   d. an open window

5. NEW ORLEANS, Louisiana (AP)—A man apparently enraged because a <u>frisbee</u> hit his parked car, shot and killed the 15-year-old boy who threw the plastic toy, police said.

The **frisbee** in this story is:
  a. a plastic toy   b. a car   c. a boy   d. police

6. MOSCOW (AP)—<u>Bugging devices</u> that could pick up anything from "a word in the living room to whispers in the bedroom or splashing water" were found in the new Soviet residential compound outside Washington, according to a report in yesterday's government newspaper Izvestia.

    The listening devices were discovered inside the walls, and included microphones, batteries, transmitters, cables and wires, Izvestia said.

The **bugging devices** in this story are:
  a. residences   c. newspaper reports
  b. whispers   d. listening devices

7.

NEW DELHI (AP)—Pakistan is reported beefing up its defenses along its 1,920 kilometer border with Afghanistan as Afghan Muslim rebels flee toward the frontier and sanctuary one step ahead of pursuing Soviet helicopter gunships and tanks.

The United News of India reported the Pakistani buildup Friday, saying seven divisions and a large armored force have been deployed along the border. The report, quoting military observers in the Afghan capital of Kabul, said all Pakistani air bases in the region were on alert.

To **beef up** in this story means:
   a. to pursue   c. to build up
   b. to report   d. to alert

8.

NEW YORK (UPI)—Television actor Cary Poe turned the tables on three muggers Sunday, flattening the trio with lightning-like kicks.

Now read quickly through the rest of the story to find out which one of the following is the best meaning of **muggers**.
   a. violent robbers   c. television actors
   b. karate fighters   d. transit police officers

The 33-year-old Poe, who plays Bill the Bartender in ABC's soap opera "One Life to Live," has black belts in karate and kung fu.

He called on his talent early Sunday morning when the men, one holding a knife, threatened him and his girl friend, Millie Vega, in Washington Square Park.

Poe told police the three men surrounded him, and one put a knife to his throat.

In a fashion more suited to a Bruce Lee movie than an afternoon soap opera, Poe let them have it, kicking the knife-wielder while he knocked out the other two men simultaneously with his fists.

As the muggers were getting their second wind, Poe said, someone yelled "freeze," and onto the scene came the cavalry in the form of two transit police officers.

They arrested two suspects identified as Vincent Acquisto, 29, and John Patures, 21. The third man fled.

They were charged with robbery and assault and Acquisto was charged with possession of a dangerous weapon.

9.

CINCINNATI (UPI)—After two weeks of crawling to the toilet in his jail cell and going for days without a shower because he couldn't reach the hardware, Anthony Pangallo—a double amputee—finally is resting in a hospital.

Now read quickly through the rest of the story to find out which one of the following best describes a **double amputee**.
   a. an unusually short person
   b. a person who has lost both legs
   c. a war hero with two medals
   d. a person who needs illegal drugs to live comfortably

> Pangallo, a 23-year-old ex-Marine with a drug dependence stemming from the accident that crippled him, was arrested December 4 on charges of filing a falsified drug prescription and receiving stolen goods. He still faces trial, but said Tuesday "my mind is at ease."
>
> Pangallo lost his legs in 1973 when he was driving a tractor and a car crashed into him. He said he received large doses of morphine during and after the amputation.
>
> "Ever since then I had a need," he said. "I had a mental depression because of losing my legs. I needed a way out. The way out was drugs."

10.
> MOSCOW (UPI)—David Ross (13) came to the Soviet Union for the Christmas holidays for a present he couldn't get at home—a special treatment he hopes will arrest the deterioration of his eyesight.
>
> The teenager, a junior high school student from Westland, Michigan, and his father have been in Moscow since Dec. 17 for special treatment at the Gelmgoltz Institute of Eye Diseases.
>
> David has had night blindness for years, but school eye tests last year showed his general vision was failing, his father, Ralph, said Tuesday.
>
> He has lost all peripheral vision and has only central vision—which means he can see what is in front of him but nothing to either side unless he turns his head.
>
> The treatment in Moscow is not designed to cure the disease. However, Soviet doctors, who have treated 19 other Americans for the same ailment, said it can arrest its progress.

The deterioration of David's eyesight mentioned in paragraph 1 means that his eyesight is _____ .

Find another word in the story that means **eyesight**.

Find another word in the story for **ailment**.

To **arrest** in paragraph one means:
   a. cure   b. capture   c. stop   d. fail

Explain this sentence: **He has lost all peripheral vision**.

Now find an English language newspaper and read several stories. Try to guess the meanings of new words before you go to a dictionary. Look up no more than five words per story.

CHAPTER

Understanding Headlines

In this chapter you will learn about the very special language of newspaper headlines.

There is an easy trick to understanding headlines in your English language newspaper—keep up-to-date on local and world news! When you pick up a newspaper and see the headline MARKOV NEEDLE CHECK, your problem is not really the language. Even a native English speaker will not understand this headline unless he knows who Markov is and the background to the story.

With a little experience you may understand many of the headlines of your local English language paper better than a native English speaker who is new to your area. Why? Because you know more about your community.

Newspaper headlines do, however, have a language of their own and it is necessary to learn about it if you want to really understand an English language newspaper.

(A) The Language of Newspaper Headlines

There are two very clear features to English newspaper headlines.

1. Headlines are almost always in the present tense.

Earthquake rocks Mexico

Bangkok fire leaves 1700 homeless

Even future events are described in present tense.

Husband to sue wife

(Husband is to sue wife)

2. Headlines generally leave out certain words, especially articles and the verb **to be**. **And** is often replaced by a comma.

Boy on cliff rescued

(A boy on a cliff is rescued)

Volunteer, terrorist killed in an ambush

(A volunteer and a terrorist are killed in an ambush)

Note that these examples look like they are in the past tense, but they are actually present tense, passive voice.

EXERCISE

Add the missing words to the following headlines.

1. **Japan to rush food, aid to Khmers**
2. **Sleepwalker puts 2 in hospital**
3. **War games planned**
4. **Islamic Press to sue UK TV firm**
5. **600 trapped by fire for 4 hours**
6. **Romulo: Big power involvement in Kampuchea dangerous**
7. **Cars, schools targets of new save-oil plan**
8. **Woman kills husband, self**

(B) *The Different Types of Newspaper Headlines*

Straight Headlines

Straight headlines simply tell you the main topic of the story. They are the most common type of headline and are the easiest to understand.

Railroad workers strike in Argentina

Man jailed for murder

Oil tanker fire

Headlines That Ask a Question

Most question headlines are not really typical questions at all. They are statements followed by a question mark. Question marks are used when:

1. The headline reports a future possibility.

Oil price to rise?

New Cabinet today?

2. There is some doubt about the truth or accuracy of the story.

Jones planned to kill Carter?

Police allowed jailbreak?

Note that this is one of the few times a newspaper headline may use a tense other than the present.

Headlines That Contain a Quotation

What people say can be as important as what they do, so it is not surprising to find a quote as a headline.

"We owe our lives to our pilot"

Mother: Let my baby go

German summit urgent—Schmidt

A quotation is another way a newspaper can begin a story with an unproven statement:

Vietnam: China planning another war

Here the newspaper itself did not accuse China of planning a war. It only reported what Vietnam claimed to be true.

Since the newspaper often prints the exact words of the person quoted, such headlines can be in any tense.

"I was not his mistress"

"We won't quit"

Quotation marks can be used for more than just indicating a direct quote. They are also used to tell you that a word is being used outside its normal meaning. For example:

NORSE 'INVASION'

You would expect this headline to introduce a war story, but it was actually about 800 Norwegians who were on a shopping trip to Scotland. The word "invasion" was used in an unusual sense and was therefore put in quotation marks.

Feature Headlines

Not all newspaper stories report major events. Some stories are included because they are highly unusual; others because they are amusing. Headlines for such stories try to be as clever as possible to catch the reader's interest. It is often necessary to read the story to understand the headline.

'Down in the mouth' news for dentists

The man who reigned over UK's Queen

The first story was about a possible vaccine for tooth decay. This would be bad news for dentists because people would have less need of their services. The second headline made clever use of the word "reign." "Reign" means "to rule" and it is used with kings and queens. Normally a queen would "reign" over the man, but in this story the man is the captain of the British ship, the Queen Mary.

Double Headlines

Double headlines are two-part headlines for the same story. They are often used for major events.

Expected to go to US

CASTRO TO FREE THOUSANDS OF PRISONERS

EXERCISE

Read the following and answer the questions.

1. Read the story and explain why "gift" is in quotation marks.

A protest 'gift' for Interior Ministry

BANGKOK (UPI)—A dead piglet was hung outside the Ministry of Interior yesterday morning in what was believed to be a *protest gesture* against an *alleged* broken promise to pig raisers made by the *Deputy* Interior Minister.

2. Read the story and explain the reason for the question mark in the headline.

China not yet one billion?

WASHINGTON (Reuter)—A government population expert back from China said he was convinced that some American *estimates* of a billion Chinese were too high.

3. Read the story and explain the use of the comma in the headline.

State, firms to pay $17 m. in damage to drug victims

TOKYO (Reuter)—A *court* yesterday ordered the Japanese Government and three drug companies to pay *damages* totaling 3,250 million yen ($17 million) to 119 victims of a nervous disease and 14 of their relatives.

62

4. Read the story and explain the headline.

Prisoner flees on govt's legs

NASHVILLE, Tennessee (AP)—A double-amputee inmate walked away from the minimum security section of the Tennessee State Penitentiary—using *artificial* legs furnished by the state.

5. Read the story and explain the use of the question mark in the headline.

Rebel chief gunned down in Sabah?

MANILA (UPI)—A Muslim *rebel* chief responsible for the killing of an Army *General* and 34 *troopers* in 1977 was himself shot dead by a *rival* rebel *commander* in the Malaysian state of Sabah, a Manila newspaper said yesterday.

Military authorities could not *confirm* the report in the Daily Express newspaper that the wily Muslim rebel leader, Usman Sali, was killed in the east Malaysian state last month.

6. Read the story and explain the use of the quotation marks in the headline.

Soviet defector 'forced' to return

WASHINGTON (UPI)—Soviet ballet dancer Yuri Stepanov, who sought *asylum* in the United States, was scheduled to fly back to Moscow Tuesday after apparently being *pressured* to go back by Soviet *officials*, a friend of the dancer said.

Stepanov, who *defected* in Rome about one month ago, had been living with friends in Washington.

A close friend of Stepanov's, Yuli Vzorov, told UPI he was convinced that the dancer had been pressured into returning to the Soviet Union.

"I think they are forcing him," Vzorov said.

7. Read the story and explain the use of the question mark in the headline.

Newspaper by satellite?

PARIS (UPI)—The International Herald Tribune said yesterday it was studying the possibility of printing its daily newspaper in Hong Kong to speed up its distribution throughout Asia.

The English-language daily, which is distributed in 143 countries, said the planned printing plant in Hong Kong would produce the newspaper from facsimile images *transmitted* directly via *satellite* from the paper's headquarters in Paris.

8. Read the story and explain the use of the question mark in the headline.

600,000 GM cars defective?

WASHINGTON (AP)—The US National Highway Safety Administration reported yesterday it was investigating possible safety-related *defects* in about 600,000 General Motors automobiles.

Ⓒ *Headline Vocabulary*

English newspaper headlines use a very special vocabulary. Here is a list to give you a fast start in learning it. You have undoubtedly seen many of the words before, but when used in headlines they may carry meanings that are unfamiliar to you.

WORD	COMMON HEADLINE MEANING	EXAMPLE
accord	agreement	**Accord possible today**
air	to make known	**TV airs 'facts' on arms delivery**
assail	to criticize strongly	**Soviets assail US on A-tests**
axe	to dismiss from a job	**Governor to axe aide?**
back	to support	**Algeria backs decision to ignore dollar**
balk	to refuse to accept	**Union balks at court order**
bar	not to allow	**Club faces shutdown for barring women**

WORD	COMMON HEADLINE MEANING	EXAMPLE
bid	attempt	**Bid to open border**
	offer	**Union rejects latest bid**
bilk	to cheat	**Clerk bilks city of $1 m.**
blast (noun)	explosion; strong criticism	**Tanker blast near Manila**
(verb)	criticize strongly; strike with explosives	**Reagan blasts democrats**
blaze	fire	**Blaze destroys factory**
cite	mention	**Management cites labor unrest for shutdown**
claim	to declare to be true	**Man claims ghost sighting**
claim (claim the life of)	to kill	**Bombs claim 40**
clash (noun)	battle; dispute	**Marine dies in clash**
(verb)	disagree strongly; fight	**Mayor clashes with city council**
cool	uninterested; unfriendly	**Hanoi cool to aid offer**
curb	limit; control	**Sunday driving curbs planned**
deadlock	a disagreement that cannot be settled	**Jury deadlock in kidnap trial**
drive	a strong well-planned effort by a group for a particular purpose	**Cancer drive exceeds goal**
due	expected	**Greek FM due today**
ease	to reduce or loosen	**1000 freed as Poland eases martial law**
eye	to watch with interest	**Women's groups eye court vote**
eve	the day before	**Violence on eve of independence**
fault	to find in the wrong	**Study faults police**
feud	dispute; strong disagreement	**Border feud danger to regional peace**
flay	accuse; criticize strongly	**US flays Soviet block**
foe	opponent; enemy	**Reagan talks with congressional foes**
foil	to prevent from succeeding	**FBI foils bid to hijack plane to Iran**
grip	to take hold of	**Cholera fear grips Japan**
gut	to destroy completely by fire	**Year's biggest fire guts 178 homes**
head off	to prevent	**President heads off rail strike**
heist	theft	**Jewel heist foiled**
hold	keep in police control; arrest	**7 held for gambling**
ink	to sign	**Thailand, Malaysia ink sea treaty**
key	very important	**Gov't. wins key vote**
kick off	to begin	**Fiery speech kicks off campaign**
lash out	criticize strongly; accuse	**Warsaw Pact lashes out at NATO missile plan**
laud	to praise	**PM lauds community spirit**
launch	to begin	**Police launch anti-crime drive**
line	position; demand	**Israel softens line**
link	connected to	**Fungus linked to mystery disease**
loom	expected in the near future	**Treaty dispute looming**

WORD	COMMON HEADLINE MEANING	EXAMPLE
loot (noun)	stolen money or goods	**Police recover loot**
(verb)	unlawful taking away of valuable goods	**Rioters loot stores**
nab	to capture	**Gang leader nabbed**
net	to take possession of; capture	**Customs check nets over $2 m.**
nod	approval	**Ministry seeks nod for oil saving plan**
office	an important government position	**Minister quits: tired of office**
opt	choose; decide	**Swiss opt to back tax for churches**
oust	to take power away from	**Voters oust incumbents**
pact	a solemn agreement	**Peace pact today?**
plea	deeply felt request	**Mother's plea: Let me see my baby**
	a statement in court indicating guilt or innocence	**Guilty pleas expected**
pledge	promise	**Union pledges support to Kennedy**
poised	ready for action	**Bolivian workers poised to strike**
poll	election	**October poll?**
	voting station	**Voters go to the polls in Japan**
post	position in government, business, etc.	**Unknown gets key Cabinet post**
probe	investigation	**Mayor orders fire probe**
prompt	to cause	**Court decision prompts public anger**
rage	to burn out of control	**Forest fire rages**
rap (noun)	accusation; charge	**Corruption rap unfair says senator**
(verb)	criticize	**Safety Commission raps auto companies.**
rock	to shock; to surprise	**Gov't. report rocks stock market**
rout	defeat completely	**Rebels routed, leave 70 dead**
row	a quarrel	**Oil price row may bring down gov't.**
rule	decide (especially in court)	**Court rules today in corruption case**
rule out	to not consider as a possibility	**Israel rules out PLO talks**
sack	dismiss from a job	**Jail chief sacked**
sack (from "ransack")	to search thoroughly and rob	**14 held for US embassy sacking**
set	decided on, ready	**Peace talks set for April**
slay	to kill or murder	**2 slain in family row**
snag	problem; difficulty	**Last minute snag hits arms talks**
snub	to pay no attention to	**Protestants snub Ulster peace bid**
soar	to rise rapidly	**Inflation rate soars**
spark	to cause; to lead to action	**Frontier feuding sparks attack**
stalemate	a disagreement that cannot be settled	**New bid to break hostage stalemate**

WORD	COMMON HEADLINE MEANING	EXAMPLE
stall	making no progress	**Peace effort in Lebanon stalled**
stance	attitude; way of thinking	**New stance toward power cuts**
stem	to prevent or stop	**Rainy season stems refugee exit**
sway	to influence or persuade	**President fails to sway union—strike set**
swindle	an unlawful way of getting money	**Stock swindle in NY**
thwart	prevent from being successful	**Honduras attack thwarted**
ties	relations	**Cuba ties soon?**
trim	to cut	**Senate trims budget**
trigger	to cause	**Killing triggers riot**
vie	to compete	**Irish top ranks vie for office**
void	to determine to be invalid	**Voting law voided by court**
vow	a solemn promise	**Police chief vows to catch kidnappers**
weigh	to consider	**Reagan weighs tax increase**

EXERCISE

Read each headline in the left column and decide what kind of a story it introduces. Match the headline with the most suitable story category in the right column.

1. _____ Old feud flares anew
2. _____ Gov't. to launch probe into disaster
3. _____ Sirica rules tomorrow on Nixon tapes
4. _____ Tuesday's poll up for grabs as Governor's support dwindles
5. _____ UK, Iceland to ink fishing pact?
6. _____ Faulty power line triggers factory blaze
7. _____ Police chief sacking politically motivated?
8. _____ Mob leader slain
9. _____ Legal row delays highway
10. _____ Parents rap school administration
11. _____ Police foil holdup
12. _____ 2 held in land swindle
13. _____ Japan pledges refugee aid increase
14. _____ Committee blasts hospital care for poor
15. _____ Seven vie for Parliament seat

a. A Dispute
b. An Arrest
c. A Murder
d. A Dismissal From Office
e. A Treaty Signing
f. A Promise
g. A Fire
h. A Decision
i. A Criticism
j. An Election
k. An Unsuccessful Crime
l. An Investigation

(D) Idioms

English newspaper headlines are full of idioms. Unfortunately a complete list of them would fill a book, so it is not possible to give you all of them here. You can usually understand the idioms in headlines, however, by reading the story that follows.

Carlo Ponti in hot water again

ROME (UPI)—Film producer Carlo Ponti, husband of actress Sophia Loren, is in trouble with the Italian courts again—this time charged with *embezzling* state funds.

The idiom in the headline is **in hot water** and its meaning is quite clear from the story. It means **to be in trouble**.

EXERCISE

All of the following stories are introduced by headlines containing idioms. Read each story to find out what the idioms mean.

1.

Refugees in dire straits

KUALA LUMPUR (Reuter)—A tramp steamer carrying 2,500 Vietnamese sent out a dramatic *appeal* for international help yesterday saying it had 500 sick people aboard, most of them children, and had run out of food and water after a 17-day *ordeal* at sea.

In dire straits in this story means:

    a. in an unknown area   c. in serious danger
    b. against the law   d. on board a ship

2.

Lid kept on Kissinger tapes

WASHINGTON (AP)—Telephone conversations Henry Kissinger had when he was *Secretary of State* and White House National *Security* Advisor are to remain secret following a ruling by the US *Supreme Court*.

To keep the lid on in this story means:

    a. to converse by telephone
    b. to record something electronically
    c. to send to court
    d. to keep secret

3.

Union call to strike falls on deaf ears

LONDON (Reuter)—Workers at a British factory yesterday *rejected* a union strike call in the latest case of what British newspapers have hailed as a new mood of realism in the country's *ailing* motor industry.

To fall on deaf ears in this story means:
- a. to receive strong support
- b. to fail to win acceptance
- c. to consider realistically
- d. to cause a serious ear problem

4.

Brezhnev on the skids?

LONDON (AFP)—The health of Soviet President Leonid Brezhnev has become so uncertain that Western *observers* believe he is no longer capable of serious *negotiation*, The Times said yesterday.

On the skids in this story means:
- a. to be in a worsening condition
- b. to be untrustworthy
- c. to be a very clever negotiator
- d. to be very unpopular

5.

Koreas to break ice after 5 years

SEOUL (UPI)—*Representatives* of South Korea will meet tomorrow with their North Korean *counterparts* at the truce village of Panmunjom for the first time in five years to discuss reunification.

To break the ice in this story means:
   a. to disagree violently
   b. to make a first move
   c. to agree to disagree
   d. to offer a proposal you know will not be accepted

6.

Let bygones be bygones, say ex-foes

ASSEMBLY POINT ROMEO, Rhodesia (Reuter)— Joshua Nkomo, *veteran* of Rhodesian Black nationalism, yesterday stood with a former *arch-foe* before his *guerrillas*, and *urged* them to work together with their *erstwhile* enemies.

In a scene that would have been unthinkable before the December 28 *ceasefire* in Rhodesia's seven-year bush war, Nkomo flew here with Gen. Sandy MacClean, Commander-in-Chief of the Army the guerrillas have been fighting.

Clasping the White general by the shoulder, Nkomo told a mixed parade of guerrillas, British *monitoring troops* and Rhodesian soldiers: "This is to show the war is over—It is essential that you and those against whom you fought should now come and work together."

The general, striking an equally *conciliatory* tone, declared: "We fought each other. That is history ... There is nothing more to fight for. All we have to do is work together to make the best country in the world."

Let bygones be bygones in this story means:
   a. Fight for what you believe in.
   b. Strike before it is too late.
   c. Forget past misunderstandings.
   d. Never give up.

Reading a Story Critically

Understanding the words of a story is not always enough. This chapter will show you how to judge whether you can believe what you read.

(A) Judging the Reliability of the Source

Read almost any news story carefully and count the facts the writer saw for himself. Often there are none at all. The news writer is almost always forced to depend on information coming from someone else—the source.

Clearly, the reader must learn to judge whether the source can be believed—whether the source is reliable. Here are six points to consider:

1. Why did the source give the information?
2. Can the source's information be checked?
3. Is the source named?
4. Could the source really have this information?
5. Where was the reporter?
6. How reliable has the source been in the past?

Why Did the Source Give the Information?

A reporter has no power to force anyone to give information, so for each news story the good reader must question why the source gave the information. The source may have a reason for not telling the complete truth. For example:

> PESHAWAR, Pakistan, March 23—Afghan rebels Friday claimed a major victory over Soviet forces, saying they killed more than 800 soldiers and destroyed six tanks in a furious two-day battle near the Soviet border.

The source of the story is the Afghan rebels. They are fighting the Soviets, so they have an interest in making it look as though they are winning victories. Therefore, you must be careful about believing their statements. Note that the writer has added a warning by using the word "claimed." The information might be true, but it is likely to be overstated and probably unreliable.

Here is a similar story, but from a different source:

> PESHAWAR, Pakistan, March 24—A major battle in Afghanistan near the Soviet border has left a large number of Russian troops dead and six tanks destroyed, travelers said Saturday.

The source is unnamed "travelers." The news writer has chosen to use this story, so he or she must think the travelers are at least probably reliable. But we still must have some doubts about the story because we don't know which side the travelers support or how much of the battle they saw.

Is the following story more reliable?

> MOSCOW, March 25—The official Soviet News Agency Tass Sunday admitted losing "some of our heroic troops" and a number of tanks last week in what it called a "treacherous attack by Afghan bandits."

Here the source is the Soviet news agency which has a clear interest in minimizing any losses. If they report the losses of their own troops and tanks, therefore, you can certainly believe it happened.

In general, the following two rules apply to sources:
1. When a source reports that something bad has happened—something against its own interests, you can believe it. In fact, you can suspect that something worse may have happened.
2. When a source reports something that is favorable to its interests, you must be suspicious. The facts may be exaggerated, or in a few cases, untrue altogether.

Can the Source's Information Be Checked?

How reliable do you think the following story is?

> MOSCOW, May 10—Soviet officials Saturday claimed resistance in Afghanistan was dying out, leaving the Soviet-supported government in "total control of all cities."

Because the source—the Soviet officials—are saying something favorable to their interests, the report cannot be considered reliable. There is another reason, however, why we must be suspicious. Outside observers cannot travel freely in Afghanistan, so the truth of the story cannot be checked.

This is another important test of a story's reliability: Can its truth be checked? If it cannot, be suspicious. Which of the following two very similar stories is more reliable?

> NEW YORK—A huge, hairy, man-like creature strolled down Fifth Avenue Friday, startling passersby and making little children cry, eyewitnesses said.

> JUMLA, Nepal—A huge, hairy, man-like creature strolled down a remote trail Friday, terrifying villagers, eyewitnesses claimed.

The sources for both of these stories say they are eyewitnesses, but the story from New York is much more reliable than the one from Jumla, because it is easier for the journalist to check on the New York story. There are always thousands of people on Fifth Avenue and such a creature would be noticed by others. But it is much more difficult to check on a story from a faraway village in Nepal. In general, stories that can be checked are more reliable than those that are difficult or impossible to check.

Is the Source Named?

The reliability of a story is also increased if the source is named since few people want to be known as liars (not true of some governments). Consider the following story:

> LAS VEGAS, June 14—Tennis star Robert "Topspin" Traeger has secretly married blue movie actress Lotta Love, sources close to Lotta's film company said today.

An interesting story, but you should become suspicious as soon as you note that the source is not quoted by name. Then you might note that the source is connected with the actress's film company—perhaps the story is in the interest of the company to gain free publicity.

But if the story reads:

> LAS VEGAS, June 14—Tennis star Robert "Topspin" Traeger has secretly married blue movie actress Lotta Love, the starlet's agent, Nathan Bottomlyne, said today.

This is more reliable because the agent has let his name be used. Still, it is not completely reliable because it is the job of agents to gain publicity for their clients.

However, when the story reads:

> LAS VEGAS, June 14—Tennis star Robert "Topspin" Traeger today announced his marriage to blue movie actress Lotta Love.

it is almost completely reliable since Traeger has made the announcement himself.

Could the Source Really Have this Information?

Another way to check reliability is to ask yourself: How much would the source really know?

> WASHINGTON, June 1—The United States has resumed secret spy flights over Cuba looking for underground missile sites, US intelligence sources said yesterday.

In a story like this it is not surprising to see the source unnamed since few intelligence agents like to be publicly known. But it is still probably reliable.

Consider this story, however.

> BRASILIA, Brazil, June 1—The United States has resumed secret spy flights over Cuba looking for underground missile sites, Brazilian intelligence sources said yesterday.

This story may be true, but it seems doubtful Brazilian intelligence sources would know very much about US activities over Cuba, so this story is probably unreliable.

Where Was the Reporter?

Check the dateline to see where the reporter was in relation to the news he is reporting.

> KAMPALA, Uganda, May 14—Victorious Tanzanian troops drove into Kampala unopposed yesterday as cheering Ugandans lined the streets to celebrate the overthrow of "Big Daddy" Idi Amin after four years of bloody misrule.

> DAR ES SALAM, Tanzania, May 14—A joint force of Tanzanian and Ugandan soldiers drove into Kampala yesterday as thousands of Ugandans cheered the fall of the bloody government of "Big Daddy" Idi Amin, field reports said.

There is not much difference between the two leads, but you should note that they have different datelines. The first one is datelined Kampala so we know that the reporter was in Kampala and close to the events he is reporting. The second story has almost the same information, but the dateline shows that the journalist was in Tanzania almost 500 miles away. The source is "field reports"—which are probably accurate, but not as reliable as a good reporter on the spot.

How Reliable Has the Source Been in the Past?

The last, but one of the most important ways for a reader to check reliability, is to remember how reliable the same source was before on similar stories. Some governments often distort or exaggerate certain stories, some are more honest.

The same thing is true of newspapers. Reporters and editors have many difficult decisions to make when they write stories. They must decide which sources to rely on and which to avoid; which facts to emphasize and which to ignore. So remember when your newspaper makes mistakes. All newspapers and all reporters make mistakes sometimes, but be careful of those that make them again and again.

EXERCISE

Read each of the following leads, identify the source, then decide how reliable the story is and why. Answers are on page 166.

1.   RED BANK, NJ, Oct 30—Supporters of Republican *candidate* Ronald Reagan Thursday distributed *pamphlets* charging Jimmy Carter with reaping *windfall profits* from "unusually high" government price supports for peanuts.

Source:
Completely reliable _____ Probably reliable _____
Unreliable _____ Why?

2.   HAVANA, Cuba—Premier Fidel Castro Wednesday *charged* that CIA agents aboard a Bermudan fishing vessel *provoked* Cuban navy ships to attack and sink the boat killing all aboard.

Source:
Completely reliable _____ Probably reliable _____
Unreliable _____ Why?

3.   TOKYO, Japan, April 22—The Japanese Minister of Trade and Industry Friday reported that the national trade *deficit* had worsened to more than US $20 billion.

Source:
Completely reliable _____ Probably reliable _____
Unreliable _____ Why?

4.   SINGAPORE, May 2—Singapore Prime Minister Lee Kuan Yew said today he will call for an extraordinary Asian *summit conference* to discuss communist *aggression* in the region.

Source:
Completely reliable _____ Probably reliable _____
Unreliable _____ Why?

5.   TOKYO, July 2—Japanese Prime Minister Ohira will travel to Singapore for a special Asian summit conference, *diplomatic sources* said yesterday.

Source:
Completely reliable _____ Probably reliable _____
Unreliable _____ Why?

6.   HONG KONG, May 17—Vietnam has handed over the former US naval base at Cam Ranh Bay to the Soviet Union for a military base, pro-Peking newspapers reported Friday quoting "reliable sources."

Source:
Completely reliable _____ Probably reliable _____
Unreliable _____ Why?

7.   BANGKOK, March 13—Chinese warplanes bombed warehouses near Haiphong *harbor* in Vietnam today causing secondary explosions among *supplies* unloaded from Soviet ships, Thai *intelligence* sources said.

Source:
Completely reliable _____ Probably reliable _____
Unreliable _____ Why?

8.   SACRAMENTO, July 4—*Incumbent* Mayor Stanley Black has had "improperly close" *financial* and social relations with *reputed* Mafia chieftains, his major *opponent* in next year's *elections* charged Thursday.

Source:
Completely reliable _____ Probably reliable _____
Unreliable _____ Why?

9.   HANOI, April 22—Chinese troops have crossed into Vietnamese territory 53 times in the past month attacking local defense posts and killing three persons, the official Vietnam News Agency said Wednesday.

Source:
Completely reliable _____ Probably reliable _____
Unreliable _____ Why?

10.   MOSCOW, Feb. 25—President Leonid Brezhnev Thursday announced the signing of a friendship *treaty* with the newly installed government of Afghanistan.

Source:
Completely reliable _____ Probably reliable _____
Unreliable _____ Why?

11. | MOSCOW, Feb. 26—President Leonid Brezhnev Friday said Soviet troops did not *invade* Afghanistan, they were invited in to help the government fight off international aggression.

Source:
Completely reliable _____ Probably reliable _____
Unreliable _____ Why?

12. | WASHINGTON, June 6—The Soviet Union has increased the number of nuclear *missiles aimed* at Western Europe, US and European intelligence sources said Wednesday.

Source:
Completely reliable _____ Probably reliable _____
Unreliable _____ Why?

Other Kinds of Newspaper Writing

In the first part of this book, you learned a lot about reading and understanding the straight news story. This is the kind of story that is most often used in the newspaper, but it is not the only kind. In this chapter you will learn about feature stories and about opinion writing, including reviews, columns, and editorials.

(A) *The Feature Story*

We have seen that most news stories follow a familiar pattern. The main points come very early in the story and less important information comes later. There is, however, another common format used in newspaper writing—the feature format.

Straight News Versus Feature

The following two stories illustrate the difference between the two patterns of writing: the straight news format and the feature format. They both contain basically the same information, but the first story is written in a straight news format, whereas the second uses a feature format.

Skim these two stories to answer the questions:

1. In which format do you find the main facts most quickly?
2. In which format do you find out the most about the personalities of the people involved in the story?
3. In which format do you find a brief summary of the facts of the situation?

Search abandoned for missing Prof

(1) MERIDA, Mexico, July 31—Local authorities today *abandoned* a massive search for missing American archeologist John Reed, who disappeared five weeks ago.

(2) Yucatan state police *commander* Luis Carillo said the search, involving helicopters, dogs and hundreds of army troops, had covered nearly 500 square miles but had turned up no *trace* of the 67-year-old professor renowned for his discoveries of Mayan temple communities in the area.

(3) "The jungle is thick and he could have gone anywhere in search of his artifacts," Carillo said.

(4) "He was old. The weather, it is very hot. Maybe he got sick or lost," the police commander said. "We now *presume* he is dead."

(5) But the professor's wife, Dr. Alana Reed, who has *vowed* to continue the search on her own, charged that the police had moved too slowly on the case and had *ignored* the possibility of *foul play*.

(6) "He knew the area too well to get lost. I believe he may have been murdered," she said. "The police, who didn't even start *investigating* until a week after he was gone, won't consider that possibility because it might reflect on the safety of the area and how they do their jobs."

(7) Dr. John Reed, who retired five years ago, was the leader of the archeological team that completed the excavation of the extensive Uximalan ruins spread 40 miles south of Merida.

(8) It is believed he was heading to those ruins when he left his hotel in Merida on June 22. Reed has been missing ever since.

Hopes dim
for missing archeologist
Fears he may have died among
the ruins he discovered

(1) MERIDA, Mexico, July 31—They met in the Mayan ruins of Uximalan. She was a student *volunteer* on a summer project and he was the eminent archeologist John Reed. In the intellectual excitement of the search for a buried Indian culture, they found an emotional excitement of their own that lasted through 32 years of marriage.

(2) But now the search is for Reed himself, missing for five weeks among the scattered jungle ruins he helped unveil.

(3) And Alana Reed fears that her husband's life, so long tied to these 1400-year-old remains of a dead empire, may have ended among them.

(4) Police and local army units have already *abandoned* the search, but Alana and a small group of friends and former associates continue to *comb* the heavy jungle south of Merida.

(5) They hope somehow, against all reason, he will be found alive and once again clap his hands in characteristic eagerness to set off for a new dig.

(6) "Even after he retired, John retained a kind of boyish enthusiasm about his work," Mrs. Reed said. "That's why he

(Continued on next page)

(Continued from p. 80)
came down here ahead of me, on his own. He has spent 35 years going through the Mayan ruins of Yucatan and he couldn't wait another week for my vacation to start."

(7) Mrs. Reed, still a fulltime professor at the Carnellon Institute of New York, fingered a Mayan shell ornament as she talked in her room at the Merida Hotel. In one corner lay the battered suitcase that her husband had left behind when he stepped out of the hotel on June 22. "We have come back here almost every year since that first summer," she said. "It was like a well to which we could always return for professional inspiration and for the renewal of personal memories."

(8) But since his retirement five years ago, the two Dr. Reeds have returned without the resources of the institute and the army of co-workers, students and diggers that participated in their early expeditions. Mrs. Reed said her husband preferred it that way.

(9) "Oh, he relished the intellectual challenge of putting all the pieces together into a coherent picture, but also he loved the excitement of digging something meaningful out of the dust with his own fingers—contributing one more piece— maybe an important one—to the puzzle."

(10) This was why he left the hotel alone that day in June—to go off with a trowel and collection bag and "potter about," as he called it, on the Uximalan ruins.

(11) The police believe he may have taken a taxi cab south of the city, but have been so far unable to find the cab driver who picked him up.

(12) They say Reed's age—67—and the hot, humid conditions of the dense jungle surrounding many of the sites may have been what killed him. They say he probably became confused and lost alone in the jungle, finally expiring from dehydration.

(13) But Mrs. Reed believes the police are reluctant to consider the possibility that her husband was the *victim* of a *crime*.

(14) "He knew the area far too well to get lost," she said.

(15) "I believe he may have been murdered."

(16) She said it would be embarrassing to have such a famous man killed in the area they were charged with protecting, so the police have refused to launch a criminal investigation.

(17) "We've found that there has been an increase in crime each time we have come back—snatching cameras or taking money at knifepoint from tourists," she said.

(18) "It was so much safer and friendlier when we first came."

(19) Mrs. Reed continues the search, going out daily with two dozen private searchers, but has begun to feel there is little hope.

(20) "You just can't live that long in the jungle. It looks so lush, but actually there is very little to eat or drink."

(21) And there have been dreams.

(22) "I have seen him, lying at the foot of a wall. His eyes are closed. He is very still. I just can't tell if he is sleeping or . . . ." Her voice trails off and she stares at the worn Mayan shell in her hands.

(23) It was a gift from her husband, a talisman of life more than ten centuries ago and now, perhaps, a relic of a life enriched by the past and now become part of it.

EXERCISE

Now read the two preceding stories more carefully and answer the following questions.

1. Compare the first paragraphs of each of the two stories. In which do you learn the most about what the story is about?
2. Feature stories use many devices to catch the reader's interest. One of the most common is the use of an unidentified pronoun at the beginning of a story. This forces the reader to

continue reading to find out who or what is being talked about. Who does **they** in paragraph one refer to? Where do you find this information?

3. In the first story, you learn the following facts about Dr. John Reed:
   a. He is a famous American archeologist.
   b. He disappeared five weeks ago in Mexico.
   c. He is 67 years old.
   d. He is married to Dr. Alana Reed.
   e. He has been retired for 5 years.
   f. He discovered Mayan temple communities and led the team that excavated the Uximalan ruins.

   What additional information do you learn about Dr. Reed in the second story? What kind of information is this?

4. Look at paragraph 7 in the feature story? Would this type of information usually be found in a straight news story? Why or why not?

5. Where must the author of the feature story have gotten his information?

The Personal Touch

The preceding feature story contains many elements commonly found in writing of this type. It is longer than a comparable straight news story. It begins more slowly and delays much of the key information until after the opening paragraph. Unlike the straight news story, it uses many devices found in short stories or novels. For example, it makes an attempt to develop the characters of the people involved, giving far more personal information than you would normally find in a straight news story. In addition, the story gives us a mental picture of the setting, and it tries to create an atmosphere or mood, helping the reader to understand the love between the wife and husband.

The next story contains many of these same elements. Read it carefully and then answer the questions at the end.

American doctor in Beirut fights fear, shells and shortages

(1) BEIRUT, Lebanon—She makes her rounds with a borrowed diving watch to take pulses in the blacked-out gloom.

(2) Shells have knocked out the emergency power generator once again and the windows are blocked with anti-*shrapnel barriers* of filing cabinets and old mattresses.

(3) She pushes back a short greying lock of hair and squats to examine a patient on the floor of the over-crowded ward.

(4) She works two eight-hour shifts per day, sleeps through shelling attacks, operates by battery powered lantern and feels more fulfilled than ever before in her career.

(5) She is Dr. Ann Worthington, a *volunteer* doctor in Beirut.

(Continued on next page)

82

(Continued from p. 82)

(6) "It got to the point where I just couldn't sit at home, watch the *carnage* on TV and then go into the hospital to tell the new interns they had to care."

(7) The 41-year-old doctor from Columbia Teaching Hospital got a leave of absence, kissed her husband and two daughters goodbye and left for Beirut.

(8) The heaviest fighting was just beginning.

(9) Soon after her arrival at West Beirut General Hospital the area became the focus of Israeli pressure on the PLO to abandon the city.

(10) Rockets hit the eight-story building twice. *Artillery shells*—no one knows from which side—knocked a corner off the ground floor and *demolished* two out-buildings. But somehow the hospital continued to function.

(11) The *victims* of the battles in West Beirut are brought first to General. "We are the front line," Dr. Worthington said. "We perform *emergency surgery* and try to get patients ready for movement to safer areas."

(12) But periods of constant shelling often make it impossible to move patients for days at a time.

(13) With one floor unuseable, the 240-bed hospital often houses over 600 patients.

(14) The overcrowding is only part of the problem.

(15) "It is the shortages that drive us to despair," she said.

(16) The fighting often makes it impossible for supplies to get through to the hospital. On this day, blood has completely run out; plasma is in critically short supply; sheets are being boiled to use as sterile dressings and doctors have to *improvise* to make up for missing drugs.

(17) "I am making decisions on treatment we would never face at home and making them in a few moments because to do nothing would mean death," she said.

(18) "Strangely, the volume of suffering doesn't deaden you." "You see so much that your mind goes into automatic drive to keep you going, but when a *patient* dies—we had a little girl so terribly burned, 80 per cent third degree, massive damage to lungs, we knew we could never save her. Somehow she lived for five days and we began to hope. When she died, we wept, we all wept."

(19) But the number of deaths in the hospital has been remarkably low despite the difficult conditions.

(20) "We know so much more about the treatment of trauma, if they get to us alive, we can almost always save them.

(21) "That's what keeps us going. Being here, able to help so many is a feeling of fulfillment greater than I've ever had before. If only we could get the fighting to stop . . . "

(22) Dr. Worthington said her family understands and sends encouragement with each letter from home.

(23) "Still they ask when I'll be back."

(24) She slumped against a mattress shrapnel guard and looked out at the darkened over-crowded ward.

(25) "It may not be for a long time."

EXERCISE

Refer to the preceding story and answer the questions.

1. Who is the **she** of the first sentence? Where do you find the answer?
2. What is the story about?
3. What do you think is the mood or atmosphere of the story?
4. List some of the details that help make that mood.
5. What do you think of the person in this story—Dr. Worthington?
6. What makes you feel this way?

A feature story is written to interest and entertain as well as to inform. For this reason, feature stories often deal with unusual subjects. In the next story, pay careful attention to the beginning, and note where the writer introduces the element of the unusual.

Mystical profits in Indonesia
Meditation a part of corporate procedure

(1) JAKARTA, Indonesia—It looked like a typical business meeting.

(2) Six men, neatly dressed in white shirts and ties filed into the boardroom of a small Jakarta company and sat down at a long table.

(3) They had decisions to make concerning a new expansion program and several personnel changes.

(4) But instead of consulting files or hearing reports, they closed their eyes and began to meditate, consulting the spirits of ancient Javanese kings.

(5) Mysticism touches almost every aspect of life in Indonesia and business is no exception.

(6) One of the meditators, Hadisiko Surono, a 47-year-old *entrepreneur*, said his weekly meditation sessions are aimed mainly at bringing the peace of mind that makes for good decision-making.

(7) But the insight gained from mystic communion with the spirits of wise kings has also helped boost the *profits* of his five companies, he said.

(8) Mysticism and profits have come together since the 13th Century introduction of Islam to Indonesia by Indian Moslem merchants.

(9) Those *devout* traders, called "Wali Ullah" or "those close to God" energetically spread both trade and religion by adapting their appeals to the native mysticism of Java.

(10) Legends attribute magic powers of foreknowledge to the Wali Ullah. These powers were believed to be gained through meditation and fasting.

(11) Businessman Hadisiko said his group fasts and meditates all night every Thursday to become closer to God and to contact the spirits of the great men of the past.

(12) "If we want to employ someone at the managerial level, we meditate together and often the message comes that this man can't hold onto money or he is untrustworthy. Or maybe the spirits will tell us he should be hired," he said.

(13) Hadisiko hastened to add that his companies also hold modern personnel management systems and that formal qualifications were essential for a *candidate* even to be considered.

(14) "But then we cross-check with meditative techniques," he said.

(15) Prospective *investments* also are considered through mystic meditation.

(16) "With the mind relaxed and open, it is easier to be objective in judging the risk of a new venture," Hadisiko said.

(17) "Meditation and contact with the wisdom of the old leaders sharpens your own insight and intuition," he said.

(18) "Then you have to apply that intuition to the information you have and work hard to be successful."

(19) One of Hadisiko's managers, Yusuf Soemado, who studied business administration at Harvard University, compared the idea of mystic management to western systems of positive thinking.

(20) "Willpower and the subconscious mind are recognized as important factors in business," he said. "Such approaches as psycho-cybernetics, Carnegie's think and grow rates, or the power of positive thinking are western attempts to tap the same higher intelligence that we contact through meditation."

(21) Hadisiko said mystic meditation has helped reverse a business slide his

(Continued on next page)

(Continued from p. 84)
companies experienced in the mid-1970's.

(22) Operating with normal business procedures, he said he lost more than $3 million in 1976 alone.

(23) "So I began to apply meditation, which I had used before only for my personal peace of mind, to the business," he said.

(24) Putting the right people in the right jobs and gaining confidence in his business decisions were the keys to a turn-around that has brought expansion and profitability, he said. The mysticism in Hadisiko's boardroom is part of a growing movement in Indonesia called "Kebatinan"—the "search for the inner self."

(25) Membership in Kebatinan cuts across religious lines and Hadisiko's group, for instance, included Moslems, a Buddhist, and several Catholics.

(26) For Hadisiko, the social contacts made through the Kebatinan movement are almost as important as any advice received from the spirit world.

(27) Among the more than 1,000 members of his immediate group who meditate each Thursday night until dawn are important bureaucrats, influential army officers, and other businessmen.

(28) Members said there was a certain trust among them that was useful in closing business deals or in winning government contracts.

(29) So the influence of Kebatinan and the profits of Hadisiko's companies continue to grow.

(30) Asked which factor accounted for the success—the mystic advice, the psychological confidence boosting or the top level contacts, Hadisiko just smiled.

(31) "In meditation we learn to be open, open to good from whatever source it comes."

EXERCISE

Refer to the preceding story and answer the questions.

1. Is it possible to tell from the first paragraph that this story will be in some way unusual?
2. In what paragraph does the writer introduce the unusual aspect of the story?
3. What was unusual about the business meeting described in the story?
4. According to Hadisiko Surono, what are the advantages of using meditation in making business decisions?
5. Is meditation the only technique used by Hadisiko's managers?
6. How is membership in Kebatinan helpful in ways other than the benefits stemming from meditation?
7. According to Yusuf Soemado, how is mystic management similar to western ways of doing business?

The Advantage of Length

The stories you have just read focus on people. Human interest is a common theme in feature writing. But features can be about almost anything. Many feature writers take advantage of one of the format's key characteristics—its extra length. This extra length allows the writer to examine complicated events that would be difficult to explain in a short news story. A straight news story is often tied to something that has just happened—it is immediate in time. But a feature story gives the news reporter a chance to write about something that has developed gradually over time, such as a trend or a change in society or the economy.

In the following story, the writer examines a trend whose effects are only now becoming clear. Note that the writer begins with a story—a common introduction in feature writing. As you read, try to figure out the writer's point in using this story and how it relates to the story as a whole.

High technology, low employment
Rising fear of the post-industrial revolution

(1) WASHINGTON — When Jane Mathesen started work at Advanced Electronics Inc. 12 years ago, she labored over a microscope, hand-welding tiny electronic *components*. She turned out 18 per hour.

(2) Now she tends the computerized machinery that turns out high capacity memory chips, far more advanced than the old components, at the rate of 2,600 per hour.

(3) Production is up, *profits* are up, her income is up and Mrs. Mathesen says the work is far less strain on her eyes.

(4) But perhaps the most significant effect of the changes at AEI was felt by the workers who are no longer there.

(5) Before the new computerized equipment was introduced, there were 940 workers at the plant. Now there are 121.

(6) A plant follow-up *survey* showed that one year after the layoffs only 38% of the released workers found new employment at the same or better wages. Nearly half finally settled for lower pay and more than 13% are still out of work.

(7) The AEI example is only one of hundreds around the country which forge intelligently ahead into the latest technology, but leave the majority of their workers behind.

(8) Its beginnings almost obscured by *unemployment* caused by the world

(Continued on next page)

(Continued from p. 86)
recession, the new technological unemployment may emerge as the great socio-economic *challenge* of the end of the 20th century.

(9) Hinde Corporation economist, Andrew Sawman, says the growth of "machine job replacement" has been with us since the beginning of the industrial revolution, but never at the pace it is now.

(10) "Out of approximately 1 billion job hours currently performed in the United States each day, more than 70 million will have been taken by machines in the next three years. In five years the number will be over 200 million and *accelerating*," Sawman says.

(11) The human costs, says Thomas Dresson of the Michigan unemployment counseling service, will be staggering. "It's humiliating to be done out of your job by a machine and there is no way to fight back," he says.

(12) "But it is the effort to find a new job that really hurts."

(13) Some workers, like Jane Mathesen, are retrained to handle the new equipment, but often a whole new set of skills is required and that means a new, and invariably smaller, set of workers.

(14) The old workers, *trapped* by their limited skills, often never regain their old *status* and employment.

(15) Dresson says "many drift into marginal areas. They feel no pride in their new work. They get badly paid for it and they feel miserable, but still they are luckier than those who never find it."

(16) The social costs go far beyond the welfare and unemployment payments made by the government. Unemployment increases the chances of divorce, child abuse, and alcoholism, a new federal survey shows.

(17) Some experts say the problem is only temporary—that new technology will eventually create as many jobs as it destroys.

(18) "The profits have to go somewhere," says economist Simon Hornegger. "Reinvested profit or *consumption* by individuals opens up the chance for new jobs, particularly in health care, education, and other services." He says "The only really job-destroying technology is technology that fails to turn a profit."

(19) But futurologist Hymen Seymour says the staggering efficiency of the new technology means there will be a simple and direct net reduction in the amount of human labor that needs to be done.

(20) "We should treat this as an opportunity to give people more *leisure*. It may not be easy, but society will have to reach a new *consensus* on the division and distribution of labor," Seymour says. He predicts most people will work only six-hour days and four-day weeks by the end of the century.

(21) But the concern of the unemployed is for now.

(22) Federally funded training, free back-to-school opportunities for laid-off workers and other schemes are in the works, but few experts believe they will be able to keep up with the pace of the new technology.

(23) For the next few years, for a substantial portion of the workforce, times are going to be very tough indeed.

EXERCISE

Refer to the preceding story and answer the questions.

1. Is this story about Jane Mathesen?
2. What is the author's point in beginning the story with her?
3. What is the trend discussed in this story?
4. What are the good points of the new technology?
5. What are the bad effects of the technology?
6. What are some possible solutions to the problems of technology and unemployment?

Opinion

Straight news stories and features seldom give you the opinion of the writer. Many newspaper articles, however, purposely state the writer's opinion. Unlike news and feature stories, they do not simply try to inform or entertain; they also try to convince. This unit looks at three such articles: the review, the column, and the editorial.

The Review

Reviews are descriptions of a book, poem, play, work of art, or film. They not only give the reader information, but also give the reviewer's reaction to his subject—sometimes in very harsh language.

Read quickly through the following review and answer the questions:

1. What is being reviewed?
2. Is the reviewer's opinion positive or negative?

Loving the unlovable

(1) LONDON—Unlike other comic strips adapted to the *stage*, "Andy Capp," which opened at the Regal Court theater last night, doesn't even try to make its hero lovable.

(2) Little Orphan Annie, Li'l Abner, Charlie Brown—they all make a pitch for affection. But Andy, even as played by quite lovable actor Courteney Thomas, throws only punches, bottles, and epithets.

(3) He is a "work-shy, beer-swilling, rent-dodging, wife-bashing, pigeon-fancying, soccer-playing, uncouth cadger," in the words of the newspaperman who conceived him.

(4) Yet Reg Smythe's comic strip appears in nearly 1,000 newspapers, wickedly exaggerating the supposed worst qualities of northern English males.

(5) The play is short on *plot*, but has some nifty one-liners.

(6) "I'm me own worst enemy," sighs Andy after a setback.

(7) "Not while my mother's alive you aren't" shouts Flo, his hard-working wife played by the ample and amply talented Sarah Hendricks.

(8) The small cast works together beautifully, and, with the sole exception of bartender Daniel Moore, who comes across a bit too proper for the 'keep in Andy's local, they are fiercely funny.

(9) The characters set up the laughs and the actors knock them off one after another with impeccable timing that accelerates the first chortles into a roar of belly laughs in each scene.

(10) The adaptation doesn't really try to be a musical play, it is determined to stick as close to the comic strip page as possible. Even the set decoration is limited to black and white.

(11) The plinkety score and short, simple lyrics reinforce the effect.

(12) In another musical the limited voices of the cast and the sparse, single piano accompaniment would provoke disappointment.

(13) But in "Andy Capp" it all fits together.

(14) You may not love Andy Capp the boozy layabout, but somehow "Andy Capp" the musical bullies and brags its way into your affections.

EXERCISE

1. Basing your answers on the preceding story, decide whether the following sentences are "fact" (F) or "opinion" (O).

   a. "Andy Capp" . . . opened at the Regal Court Theater last night.

   b. The small cast works together beautifully.

   c. Reg Smythe's comic strip appears in nearly 1,000 newspapers.

   d. The play is short on plot, but has some nifty one-liners.

   e. Bartender Daniel Moore . . . comes across a bit too proper.

   f. The set decoration is limited to black and white.

   g. In another musical the limited voices of the cast and the sparse, single piano accompaniment would provoke disappointment. But in "Andy Capp" it all fits together.

   h. The musical bullies and brags its way into your affections.

2. Look back at the sentences you marked "opinion." For each item, decide whether the opinion is "positive" or "negative."

The Column

Newspaper columns also express opinions. Writers of such columns are sometimes famous and influential, so their columns are often headed by their own pictures. Each columnist has his own style. Some try to be funny. Others are very serious. To really appreciate a column you should read it often and try to understand the basic attitudes of the writer. Remember, unlike a news writer, a columnist does not have to present the facts in a balanced or objective way.

Read the following political column carefully and decide as best you can what the columnist's political position is. By way of background, in American politics, liberals generally favor a strong government role in the society and the economy. Conservatives favor a reduced role.

The Wright side
By Samuel L. Wright

(1) For a Democratic President, Carl Arling has come pretty close to making the right *diagnosis* of what *ails* our economy—lack of *investment*. But his new economic plan seems like a quack *cure.*

(2) His elaborate scheme for investment credits, government funding for high technology research, the technological skills development program, and revitalizing the science and math programs of our schools may end up worse than no cure at all. It could just bring on more of the government interference that has been holding our businessmen back for so long.

(3) Arling hasn't said how he is going to *finance* the plan, but close aides have

(Continued on next page)

(Continued from p. 89)
been telling the Congress privately it will require federal borrowing and higher taxes.

(4) They say the new plan will generate so much new *revenue* that the new taxes, which will be phased in after a two-year delay, will easily pay off the debt.

(5) What they don't say is what happens if revenues don't go up as fast or as far as the President expects. Well, the answer to that is clear—more government borrowing, financed by speeding up the printing presses down at the mint. So we'll be back in the same fevered *inflation* that it took the painful medicine of a four-year recession to cool.

(6) Anyway, there should be no mystery about encouraging more investment. You just allow the businessman to produce a product without *interference*, give him *access* to a market for it, and then let him keep most of the proceeds.

(7) That means the government should stop its bureaucrats from trying to tie down our businesses with regulations and paperwork. It means that government should start doing what it is supposed to do—standing up to foreign governments and breaking through those *trade barriers* erected often by our closest allies. And it means that taxes should be CUT, not raised. The profit *motive* can only motivate someone if he knows he'll be allowed to keep his profits.

(8) There's no patent on this brand of medicine, it's just hard for a weak stomached government to keep down.

EXERCISE

Refer to the preceding story and answer the questions.

1. Does the columnist generally agree or disagree with President Arling's idea of what is wrong with the economy?
2. Is the "quack cure" mentioned in paragraph one something good, or bad?
3. What does this "quack cure" involve?
4. What does the columnist say would be the result of this cure?
5. What does he think the proper role for government is?
6. Do you think the columnist is more conservative or more liberal than the President?

The Editorial

Another kind of opinion writing in the newspaper is the editorial. This is actually an expression of the opinion of the editors of the newspaper themselves. In their news stories, they try to present the facts in a fair and balanced way, but in the editorial they can tell you what they think of that news.

Editorials are found on a special page which usually contains opinion columns as well. The page may also contain letters to the newspaper from the readers. The editorial (or editorials) will generally be found on the upper left side of the page.

Editorials differ from newspaper to newspaper and from writer to writer, so it is not possible to describe the typical editorial. Most editorials do, however, contain at least some of the following elements:

1. An introduction of the topic that identifies the problem being discussed and gives the reader some background about the subject.
2. Alternative solutions to the problem that the editorial does not agree with.
3. Evidence supporting the conclusion favored by the writer.
4. A clear expression of the editorial opinion, often with a suggestion of what action should be taken.

Skim the editorial to answer the questions:

1. What problem is being discussed?
2. What editorial opinion is being expressed?

In most editorials, the problem will come toward the beginning and the opinion of the paper toward the end. When you finish, read the editorial more carefully and look for the other elements mentioned in the preceding list.

The President's plan

(1) President Arling has put his long awaited economic restructuring program before the Congress. It provides a coordinated program of *investment credits*, research *grants*, education reforms, and tax changes designed to make American industry more competitive. This is necessary to *reverse* the economic slide into unemployment, lack of growth, and trade *deficits* that have plagued the economy for the past six years.

(2) The most liberal wing of the President's party has called for stronger and more direct action. They want an incomes policy to check *inflation* while federal *financing* helps rebuild industry behind a wall of protective *tariffs*.

(3) The Republicans, however, decry even the *modest*, graduated tax increases in the President's program. They want tax cuts and more open markets. They say if federal money has to be injected into the economy, let it be through defense spending.

(4) Both these alternatives ignore the unique nature of the economic problem before us. It is not simply a matter of markets or financing. The new technology allows vastly increased production for those able to master it. But it also threatens those who fail to adopt it with permanent second-class citizenship in the world economy. If an industry cannot lever itself up to the leading edge of technological advances, then it will not be able to compete effectively. If it cannot do this, no amount of government *protectionism* or access to foreign markets can keep it profitable for long. Without the profits and experience of technological excellence to reinvest, that industry can only fall still further behind its foreign competitors.

(5) So the *crux* is the technology and that is where the President's program has focused. The danger is not that a plan will not be passed; it is that the ideologues of right and left will *distort* the bill with *amendments* that will blur its focus on technology. The economic restructuring plan should be passed *intact*. If we fail to restructure our economy now, we may not get a second chance.

EXERCISE

Refer to the preceding editorial and answer the questions.
1. What is the problem the editorial discusses?
2. Why did the President introduce his plan?
3. Who is proposing alternative ideas for helping the economy?
4. What are these alternatives?
5. Why does the editorial writer think the President's plan is a good one?
6. What does he want the Congress to do?

Now try reading editorials in an English language newspaper. For each one, try to answer these questions:

1. What is the problem the editorial discusses?
2. What does the editorial writer want to happen?

PART TWO

High-Frequency
News Stories

How to Use Part Two

The stories that follow were written especially for this book to give you an idea of the type of stories and the vocabulary you can expect to find in an English language newspaper. All of the stories are fictional—they do not report actual events—but they are typical of the newspaper style. They will give you an excellent background for the newspaper reading you do in the future.

When you read these stories, follow the method described in this book.

1. Scan the story to find out the topic and the main points.
2. Read the opening paragraph carefully and form questions that you would like the story to answer.
3. Finish the story and try to answer your questions. Form new questions and try to answer them.
4. Try to guess the meanings of unfamiliar words wherever possible. Picture the story in your mind. Look for synonyms and explanations.
5. Remember that the meanings of italicized words can be found in the glossary. Do not overuse the glossary, however. Look up only those words that are necessary to your understanding of the story. Later, when you have finished and understood the story, you may want to go back and look up additional words.
6. When you finish a story, try to find similar stories in a newspaper. You should recognize much of the vocabulary. If possible, follow a story for several days or even weeks. Note how quickly the vocabulary becomes familiar.

Politics and Government

① Party convention

DETROIT, July 22—Colorado *Senator* Carl Arling last night won the *Democratic Party nomination* for president and immediately named Michigan Governor Bartley Depointe as his *running mate*—the first black ever on a major party presidential *ticket*.

Riding a *surge* of six consecutive *primary* victories going into the *convention*, Arling won his first *ballot* nomination even more easily than expected, piling up 2,789 votes to 1,321 for five different regional, favorite son, and single-issue *dark horse candidates*.

Gov. Depointe, who controlled nearly 600 *votes* won in midwestern state *caucuses*, released his *delegates* before the balloting began to assure Arling's easy nomination.

(Continued on next page)

95

(Continued from p. 95)

Depointe, credited with *masterminding* the economic *revival* of his state, was not an unexpected choice since his *appeal* to *urban*, eastern, and midwestern voters and minorities nationwide provided a neat balance to Arling's popularity among *rural*, western, and conservative Democrats.

The Michigan governor downplayed the importance of his being the first black candidate for vice president.

"I think the *electorate* is politically *mature* enough to look beyond a man's skin color and see him for what he says and does."

Arling and Depointe will run on a party *campaign platform* described as *liberal* on social *issues*, but *conservative* on economic *policy*.

One of the most *controversial* planks in the platform calls for a *comprehensive*, nationwide *medical welfare system*.

Answer the following questions as completely as possible and then check the answers on page 170 in the answer key.

1. Who won election as president of the United States?
2. Where does Carl Arling come from?
3. Why was Bartley Depointe made Arling's running mate?
4. How did Arling win many of his votes at the convention?
5. Why did Depointe have control of 600 delegates?
6. What kind of policies will the Arling-Depointe ticket propose during the campaign?

② Political campaign

NEW YORK—With less than two weeks before the presidential *election, Democratic candidate* Sen. Carl Arling has made significant gains against Republican Vice President Lawrence Letterman and now *trails* by less than 5% in the latest *polls*.

Analysts said the latest surge by Arling corresponded to the announcement last week of a further increase in the nation's *trade deficit* and another rise in *unemployment*.

If the *trend* continues, the two candidates will be in a virtual *dead heat* by election day, the analysts said.

A Daily Times *commissioned* poll with a computer-selected *sampling* of 5,000 eligible voters showed Letterman leading by 45.4% to 40.7%.

Arling and *running mate* Gov. Bartley Depointe continued to hit hard at the failure of the Republican *administration* to halt the *deterioration* of US industrial *competitiveness* abroad.

Depointe *campaigned* extensively in the deep south where he projected a *moderate image* that *focused* on his

record of successfully *reviving* industries in his home state, Michigan.

Depointe promised to set up a federal program to restructure the economy of the newly industrialized south and put the unemployed back to work.

The unspoken *issue* of the campaign remains voter reaction to Depointe as the first black named to a major party presidential *ticket*. *Pollsters* said there appeared to be no significant regional patterns so far with the Democratic ticket headed by a conservative from a rural state and the Republican ticket led by the *articulate* and liberal vice president.

Letterman continued to *pursue* his *strategy* of attacking Arling's voting record on urban issues on his *swing* through the industrial northeast.

He dismissed Depointe's urban expertise as "irrelevant."

"It's the president who makes the policies and it will do no good to our *ailing* cities if we have a Colorado cowboy *holding the reins*," he said.

Arling dismissed the charges as "sophisticated *mudslinging*."

Answer the following questions as completely as possible and then check the answers on page 170 in the answer key.

1. Who won election as president of the United States?
2. Who is the Republican candidate for president?
3. According to the poll, what percentage of voters will vote for Letterman?
4. What seems to be the issue that is allowing Arling to gain on Letterman?
5. Why is the vice-presidential candidate, Depointe, important?

(3) Election result

WASHINGTON, D.C.—Democrat Carl Arling Thursday *upset* Vice President Lawrence Letterman, taking 52.4% of the *popular vote* to become the 43rd president of the United States.

The come-from-behind Democratic victory also made Gov. Bartley Depointe the nation's first black vice president *elect*.

The Democratic ticket swept the large industrial states of both north and south to pile up 308 electoral votes to 230 votes for Republican candidate, Vice President Lawrence Letterman.

The Democrats also regained control of the *Senate* and the *House of Representatives* for the first time in eight years.

"This gives us the people's *mandate* for a *radical* change in our industrial *policies*, to restructure our economy so it can provide jobs and income for all," Arling said in his victory statement.

Arling said he would start work immediately to select a *cabinet* and a *transition team*.

It was a *landslide* win by more than 12% in California that finally gave Arling a *majority* in the *electoral college*.

The pattern of the voting was not *regional*, analysts said. Everywhere in the country Letterman did well in rural areas and wealthy *suburbs* while Arling scored heavily in the inner cities.

The battle was closest among the middle-class suburbs where Arling's call for a restructured, high technology industrial base seemed to have great voter *appeal*.

Analysts said that the *deteriorating* economy and a *lackluster* performance by Letterman in a nationally televised debate also worked to Arling's favor. Although he started well behind the better known Letterman, the Democratic candidate gained *momentum* throughout the campaign to pull ahead of the Republican on election day.

Answer these questions and check your answers against those on page 170 in the answer key.

1. Who won election as president of the United States?
2. Who led at the beginning of the presidential campaign?
3. What percentage of the electoral votes did Arling win?
4. What were some of the reasons the Democrats won?
5. Where did Letterman gain most of his support?
6. Did the Republicans win a majority of the seats in the House of Representatives?

④ Debate in the Legislature

WASHINGTON, D.C., Aug. 21— *Debate* on the *controversial medical welfare bill* is set to *wind up* today in the *House of Representatives* with supporters claiming they have enough votes for passage.

But *opponents* of the law have threatened to propose a series of *amendments* from the floor to change the *legislation* they claim will "*subsidize* murder and *socialize* medicine."

Administration *sources* said President Carl Arling will *veto* the *bill* if "amendments prevent this country from achieving a just and effective system of health care."

House Majority Leader Warren Williams said the welfare law is unlikely to pass without some changes. "But most of the stiffest opposition is to nonessential portions of the bill," he said.

"We already have enough votes to pass the heart of it," he said.

The most controversial part of the 603-page bill designed to improve the American health system, deals with federal *subsidies* to hospitals serving *poverty-stricken* areas.

Opponents of the bill insist that no hospitals or *clinics* performing *abortions* be *eligible* for *federal funds*.

A *vociferous* and well-organized pressure group led by the "Right-to-Life" Organization has *waged a battle* that kept the legislation *bottled up* in committee for two years.

Chief *lobbyist* for the group, Kate Hilburn, argues, "abortion is *legalized* murder and we don't want our tax dollars paying for it."

She said she expected a lively debate that would convince *legislators* that the "worst parts" of the law have to be changed.

Lobbying in favor of the controversial *provisions* is an equally *ardent coalition* of *women's liberation* groups and *liberal* doctors.

Showing surprising *talent* for political *arm twisting*, the group organized a large outpouring of letters in support of the bill from the districts of committee members. The bill then squeezed through the conservative House Ways and Means Committee by one vote.

"Now that the bill is out of committee and *on the floor*, I am confident it will pass without major amendments," House speaker, Philip "Flip" Thompson said after he and Democratic Whip, Cyril Fitch *tallied* support for the bill.

But he warned that the legislation still faced strong opposition in the Senate.

"Eventually there will have to be a *compromise* in the joint House-Senate sub-committee before we get the kind of health system this country needs and deserves," Thompson said.

Give full answers to these questions and check them against those on page 171 in the answer key.
1. Did the medical welfare bill become law on Aug. 21?
2. Where was the bill being considered?
3. Why do some people oppose the bill?
4. After the bill is approved by the House of Representatives, will it go into immediate effect?
5. Do opponents of the bill want to defeat it completely, or make changes in it?
6. What is the medical welfare law designed to do?

⑤ Vote of confidence

JERUSALEM, Jan. 24—*Prime Minister* Magen Sterten narrowly won a *vote of confidence* in the Israeli *Parliament* yesterday over his government's decision to open peace talks with the People's Republic of Palestine.

Sterten's *fragile* five-party *coalition* held together despite strong pressure from the conservative opposition, who have called for a final *military* solution to the border problems that have *plagued* the two countries since the formation of the Palestinian state three years ago.

The *charismatic* Sterten, a former armed forces *commander*, reminded Parliament he had three times led Israeli attacks through the land now *occupied* by the new state.

"I would attack them thirty times more if I thought that would solve our problems," he said.

"But now is the time for the *negotiator*, not the soldier," he said. "Now is the time for a peaceful, political solution. If we don't grasp it now, it may never come again," Sterten warned.

Sources in the Prime Minister's *party* said the emotional speech had stopped a number of possible *defections* from the coalition and enabled the government to win a narrow seven-vote victory.

In the fierce, three-hour debate that preceded the vote, the opposition parties had called on Sterten to *dissolve* Parliament and bring the issue of the negotiations to the people in a general election or *referendum*.

Analysts said the vote of confidence had made the *prospects* for long term peace in the Middle East brighter than they have been for 20 years.

Answer the following questions and then check page 171 in the answer key.
1. Will Israel have a general election or referendum soon?
2. How many political parties share in the government of Israel?
3. Who voted in Israel on Jan. 23?
4. Why did the opposition want the prime minister to dissolve Parliament?
5. Has the government decided to hold peace negotiations with the People's Republic of Palestine?

Summit meeting

VIENNA, Austria, Aug. 14—US President Carl Arling and Soviet President Nikolai Kosenko today *wound up* their three-day *summit conference* with a joint *communique* that promised "cooperation instead of *confrontation.*"

After signing the second *Strategic Arms* Reduction *Treaty*—START II—yesterday, the two leaders discussed ways to reduce mutual distrust and *antagonism* that still threaten the formal

ratification of the treaty in both capitals.

A spokesman said the discussion made significant progress and a joint statement issued at the end of the first US-Soviet summit meeting in 16 years said: "the two sides agreed to move ahead in *mutual* cooperation instead of confrontation in all fields."

But at the same time *conservatives* in the US Congress called for a renegotiation of the complex treaty which sets out

(Continued on next page)

(Continued from p. 99)
a 15-year step-by-step schedule for the *dismantling* of nuclear tipped *missiles*.

Sources in the Soviet delegation said the treaty also faced fierce *opposition* from a *hardline faction* within the Communist Party leadership. They noted that Defense Minister Gen. Semyon Radischin, scheduled to attend the conference, had pulled out at the last moment complaining of ill health.

President Arling, elected to office just under a year ago, said the conclusion of the arms reduction *accord* had been his top *priority* in foreign policy.

"It is now *imperative* that the *momentum* for peace, once regained, never again be surrendered to the forces of *ultra-nationalism* and hatred."

President Kosenko said the gains from the treaty would not be limited to nuclear arms reduction.

"This increase in trust and understanding will be felt across the entire spectrum of *issues* facing us."

Conference sources said that the two new leaders had developed good personal relations in their three days of *intensive* talks, sometimes meeting for key *sessions* with no *agenda* and no officials other than their interpreters present.

New *initiatives* are expected as a result of the private talks on trade and technical cooperation, the Soviet occupation of Afghanistan, and the US trade *embargo* against Cuba, the sources said.

Analysts said the personal *diplomacy* of the summit had lifted US-Soviet relations to their highest point in two decades.

Answer the following questions and then check page 171 in the answer key.

1. Who met at the summit conference in Vienna?
2. Was the meeting attended by the Soviet defense minister?
3. Did the talks make progress on improving relations between the two countries?
4. What problems remain for the Strategic Arms Reduction Treaty?
5. What does the treaty do?
6. What else was discussed besides the treaty?
7. Is the treaty now legally in effect?

 # Political ouster

MOSCOW, Dec. 15—Soviet President Nikolai Kosenko has been *ousted* from all party and government positions in a *stunning* political *purge* of moderate leaders by a *hardline faction* in the ruling Communist Party.

An official government announcement said the president had "retired to his country home to allow more vigorous leadership to guide the country through the current *crisis*."

The announcement said the decision to remove Kosenko after less than two years in office was taken at an emergency meeting of the Communist Party central committee two days ago.

Kosenko also *resigned* as party first secretary and from government council of ministers, it said.

Diplomatic *sources* said the victorious hardliners, led by Defense Minister Gen. Semyon Radischin and KGB secret service chief, Lazar Kaganovich, *consolidated* their grip on power with the *arrests* of more than 500 *moderate* officials this morning.

Analysts said the political *upheaval* came after more than two months of (Continued on next page)

(Continued from p. 100)
bitter debate at top levels of the party over *military reverses* in Afghanistan, the *sagging* economy and the newly signed *Strategic Arms* Reduction *Treaty*— START II.

Soviet government sources said a new government would be formed with a collective leadership. Technocrats will be named to the *premiership* and to head most of the ministries, they said, but most power will lie with Radischin and Kaganovich.

The *emergence* of the tough defense minister may signal the end of the "peaceful coexistence" with the west policy *revived* by Kosenko. It is almost certain to mean the reversal of the gradual *withdrawal* of Soviet *troops* from Afghanistan where the communist government has shown it is still incapable of standing on its own. Kaganovich is said to have strongly opposed the withdrawal begun last year.

Harsh measures are also expected in industries *bogged down* by what Kaganovich has called "economic *subversion* and industrial *treason*" on the part of workers demanding higher pay and shorter working hours.

Answer the following questions and then check page 171 in the answer key.
1. What happened to Soviet President Nikolai Kosenko?
2. Who is the new president?
3. What happened to moderate officials?
4. Who seems to be in charge of the government now?
5. Why was there a change in the Soviet leadership?
6. What effects are expected from the ouster of Kosenko?

⑧ International conference

CAIRO, Egypt, Dec. 17 — The *non-aligned movement* today closed its *annual foreign ministers' conference* with an offer to *forgo* the development of all nuclear weapons if the *superpowers* will speed up reductions in their own nuclear *arsenals*.

The 92-nation movement also set up a *mediation panel* to help *negotiate* an end of the second Iran-Iraq war, and passed a series of resolutions marking its renewed unity after more than 20 years of *disputes*.

The members of the nonaligned conference, including nuclear powers India, Argentina, Pakistan, and Egypt, pledged to forgo all development of their nuclear capabilities if the United States and the Soviet Union *step up* the *time table* agreed last August for *strategic arms* reductions.

Since the four countries were on the *verge* of producing deliverable nuclear weapons, the nuclear *resolution* was seen as more than just a *goodwill gesture*.

Diplomats in Moscow and Washington said the resolution would be studied carefully to see if it could be helpful as the basis for renewed talks.

The proceedings of the movement were remarkable for their lack of *controversy* and *reaffirmation* of the principles of nonalignment.

The meeting also *resolved*:
• to admit the new *neutralist* government of Cambodia as a full member.
• to back Third World calls for *access* to the new energy technology.
• to welcome the Soviet troop *withdrawals* begun last year in Afghanistan.

Answer the following questions and then check page 172 in the answer key.

1. What offer did the nonaligned movement make on nuclear weapons?
2. How many nonaligned countries have nuclear weapons?
3. What two members of the movement are fighting a war?
4. What will the movement do to try to end the war?
5. Was the nonaligned movement in favor of the Soviet invasion and occupation of Afghanistan?
6. Which country is the newest member of the movement?

 9

State visit

BONN, West Germany, July 7—On the first *state visit* to Germany by a French leader in nearly ten years, President Pierre Lemontre called for a stronger European *role* within the Atlantic *Alliance.*

In reply to a *banquet toast* by West German Chancellor Kurt Schneider, the French president declared that the world needed a strong and independent Europe.

He *reaffirmed* France's *commitment* to the North Atlantic Treaty Organization, which includes the United States, Canada, and most of the western Europe, warning that the *allied* nations must take action to *counter* the growing *military* strength of Soviet forces in eastern Europe.

Lemontre began the first visit to Germany by a French head of state since a trip by then President Valery Giscard d'Estaing more than nine years ago by meeting Schneider for wide-ranging discussions.

Accompanied by close *aides* and the French ambassador to Germany, Lemontre also spent an afternoon relaxing with German leaders at Schneider's country retreat.

Aides said the two European leaders *touched on* the situation in the middle east, the continuing *withdrawal* of Soviet troops from Afghanistan and the effect of the recently *ratified* US-Soviet *Strategic Arms* Reduction *Treaty* on European *defenses.*

They said Lemontre pressed Schneider to support calls for *negotiations* between Israel and the People's Republic of Palestine. He also asked Schneider to consider a swift *normalization* of diplomatic *relations* with the newly formed republic. Schneider is considering the *proposals,* the sources said.

The French president was said to have denied that the *republic* was pro-Soviet.

"The French position is that this government is now in *de facto* control of its territory and that it will only turn to the Communists if it receives no support from the West," said one official who asked to remain *anonymous.*

After a series of ceremonial functions Lemontre will again meet Schneider at his home before returning to France.

Answer the following questions and then check page 172 in the answer key.

1. Who is the head of state of France?
2. Is France a member of the North Atlantic Treaty Organization?
3. Has Schneider supported Israeli-Palestinian negotiations?
4. What government is described as being in de facto control of its territory?
5. Why must the allied nations improve their military strength according to Lemontre?

Disasters

 # Storm

MIAMI, Sept. 16—*Hurricane* Eva, with winds *gusting* to 110 miles per hour struck the Florida coast yesterday, killing at least four persons and *wreaking widespread havoc.*

The eye of the hurricane, the worst *tropical* storm to hit the area in seven years, passed within 25 miles of Miami before *veering* out to sea again, the national *weather bureau* said.

Meteorologists said heavy seas, high *tides,* and strong winds would continue for several days in the *wake* of the hurricane.

Winds clocked up to 110 miles per hour near the center ripped roofs off dozens of houses, whipped up huge waves along the coast, and knocked down hundreds of power lines, blacking out much of the Miami area.

More than 30,000 people along the coast have been ordered to *evacuate* their homes in flood-*prone* areas.

Emergency *volunteers labored frantically* to hold back rising tides with *levees* of sand bags, but many low-lying areas have already been *inundated.*

No official *casualty toll* has been *made public,* but police and hospital officials report at least four people have died storm-related deaths so far and many more have been reported missing.

Two teenaged boys were reported *drowned* after their 18-foot motorboat *capsized* in Biscayne Bay near Fisher Island. A 23-year-old Fort Lauderdale woman and an 82-year-old man from Ojus died in Miami General Hospital from head injuries caused by wind-blown *debris.*

Emergency wards in the city's hospitals were crowded with *victims* of the storm, most suffering only minor injuries.

But officials said dozens of people were reported missing, mostly from boats in the bay, and the death toll was expected to rise.

Answer the following questions and then check page 172 in the answer key.

1. What is the name of the hurricane?
2. How many people have died from the hurricane?

3. Why did the volunteers work with the sand bags?
4. How fast was the hurricane moving?
5. How fast were the winds of the hurricane moving?
6. What did the hurricane winds do?

② After the storm

MIAMI, Sept. 17—Most of the Florida *coast* was declared a *federal disaster* area yesterday as the death toll from Hurricane Eva rose to 17 and property *damage* was estimated at more than $800 million.

National Guardsmen moved in to prevent *looting* and to help in continuing *rescue* operations.

Flood waters were *subsiding* in most areas, but 50-mile-per-hour winds and 25-foot waves continued to lash the coast.

Governor Arnold Sawcross toured the disaster area in a helicopter and told newsmen "the *devastation* is beyond belief."

"It will take years for us to rebuild," he said.

But the governor also said that hurricane *victims* and local governments everywhere south of Daytona Beach were *eligible* for federal disaster *relief funds*.

The Disaster Control Center said that the death *toll* had risen to 17 people killed in the storm with more bodies expected to be found as rescue workers searched the *wreckage* of seaside homes hit by wind and waves.

Another 179 people were injured seriously enough to require *hospitalization*.

Property damages were expected to exceed $800 million, the center said.

About 5,000 homes were seriously damaged by coastal flooding. Electrical power was still not completely *restored* to many areas because of *massive damage* to power poles and lines.

Thousands of private pleasure boats were believed sunk or *capsized* along the once *elegant* Miami waterfront.

Governor Sawcross called it "the worst natural *catastrophe* to hit the state in two *decades*."

Answer the following questions and then check page 172 in the answer key.
1. Was the storm over by Sept. 17?
2. How many people had to stay in the hospital for treatment of their injuries?
3. How much damage did the hurricane do?
4. What will help the hurricane victims to rebuild after the damage?
5. Why did the National Guardsmen move into the disaster area?

③ Accident

BOULDER, Colorado, Feb. 2—A *jam-packed* busload of skiers last night crashed head-on into a tractor-trailer truck and *plunged* into a mountain *ravine*, killing 17 people and seriously *injuring* 32 others.

Police at the scene of the accident said

they pulled dozens of victims from the *crumpled wreckage* of the bus.

Others had been flung out of the *demolished* bus and *strewn* over the hillside.

The officer *investigating* the *tragedy*
(Continued on next page)

(Continued from p. 104)

said the bus was *overtaking* a small van on an icy curve when it *collided* with the truck.

The slightly injured truck driver told police he tried to *swerve* but *skidded* on the icy road into the bus. He said the force of the *impact* knocked the empty truck across the *shoulder* of the road into a *ditch* where it overturned.

Survivors said the bus driver pulled out to pass the van when the slower moving vehicle refused to yield the right of way.

Suddenly the truck came around the bend and plowed into the bus, they said.

The bus driver lost control of the bus and it *hurtled* off the road into a steep ravine, flipping over twice before ramming into a tree.

Ten of the passengers and the bus driver were killed *instantly*. Six others were declared dead on arrival at the hospital. A total of 50 victims were treated for injuries, hospital officials said.

Police have not yet *identified* all the dead and said several bodies were *mangled* beyond recognition.

Officials said it was the worst traffic accident in the state in five years.

Answer the following questions and then check page 172 in the answer key.

1. Where did the accident occur?
2. How many people were hurt in the crash?
3. Which two vehicles collided?
4. What happened to the truck?
5. What happened to the van?
6. What happened to the bus?
7. Who do you think was most at fault in the accident?

Fire

LONDON, Sept. 23—*Flames* raced through the 16-story Luxury Hotel in Kensington yesterday in a pre-dawn fire that killed at least 17 people and *injured* dozens more.

Firemen fought the *blaze* for more than eight hours, fearful it would spread to nearby buildings, before finally bringing it under control.

Smoke from the intense flames billowed upward as people *trapped* in the hotel screamed for help.

One group of hotel guests said they had to smash through a jammed *emergency exit.* Others, unable to reach fire escapes, leaped three stories to the ground when smoke and flames reached them before firemen or ladders could.

Officials said at least 17 people were confirmed dead in the *holocaust* and feared the death *toll* could rise as *rescue* workers *comb* the *charred rubble* of the once elegant hotel.

Hospital *authorities* said 259 people

have been treated for smoke inhalation and burns. At least 43 of those have been *hospitalized*—many with *second and third degree burns.*

Six people were reported in *critical condition.*

Witnesses said the blaze started when a canister of *inflammable* cooking gas burst into flames in the kitchen of the hotel restaurant.

Hotel employees were unable to *extinguish* the fire which quickly spread, *touching off* more stored cooking gas in a series of *blasts.*

Even before fire *alarms* went off the explosions *roused* most of the hotel guests. Some of them *stampeded* for the main exit next to the blazing restaurant, but then had to *retreat* when they found it *engulfed* in flames.

Most finally escaped through emergency exits in the rear of the building.

The fire burned for more than five hours, *gutting* the entire structure.

Answer the following questions and then check page 173 in the answer key.
1. What burned down?
2. What caused the fire?
3. What delayed some people from escaping from the hotel?
4. How many people still might die from their injuries in the fire?
5. How much of the hotel was burned?

⑤ Earthquake and volcano

MEXICO CITY, May 29—A *massive earthquake* and *volcano eruption* rocked a tiny Mexican island yesterday, leveling the island's three fishing villages and killing at least 35 people.

Seismologists said the quake at Clarion Island, 650 miles west of the Mexican mainland, has *triggered* a huge *tidal wave*, spreading out from the island.

Government officials said they fear the death *toll* will rise over 100 with many more people left homeless by the *disaster*.

Government reports said the earth-quake, which *registered* 7.9 on the *Richter Scale*, struck the island with 980 *inhabitants* early yesterday morning, reducing most buildings on the island to *rubble* within moments.

The Mexico City Seismology Institute said the *epicenter* of the quake was located exactly at the island.

The *shocks* apparently set off an eruption of the island's long *dormant* Mount Gallegos volcano, the institute said.

The massive *destruction* has *paralyzed* rescue efforts by *authorities* on the island.

(Continued on next page)

(Continued from p. 106)

Rescue teams from off the island have been *hampered* by the *tidal wave* and a huge pall of smoke and *ash* thrown up by the volcano that has *obscured* the island's only airstrip.

The first *casualty* reports saying that 35 people had *perished* are almost certainly incomplete, officials said, since dozens of people are still unaccounted for.

Seismologists said they expect a series of sharp aftershocks to send more *tremors* through the area, causing more *damage* and increasing the flow of *molten lava* that has already poured down the mountainside halfway to the island's main village.

Officials said they were going to organize a *sealift* to *evacuate* as many people from the island as possible.

Answer the following questions and then check page 173 in the answer key.
1. Did an earthquake hit Mexico City?
2. What did the earthquake cause?
3. Where is the island?
4. What is delaying rescue efforts from the mainland?
5. What dangers still face the people on the island?
6. What do government officials want to do to help?

Drought

TOPEKA, Kansas, July 16—A two-month-long *drought* through most of the Great Plains is seriously *threatening* the fall harvest of wheat and corn, *agriculture* department experts said yesterday.

Regional representative George Haden said the federal government has already *allocated* more than $15 million in *emergency funds* for *irrigation* to prevent a complete *crop* failure.

Weather *forecasts* for the rest of the month, however, indicate no *relief* for farmers who have suffered through *scorching* summer temperatures with less than 10 percent of normal rainfall.

"The drought has already *jeopardized* more than $3 billion in corn and wheat crops and the *damage* could be even worse if we don't get some rain soon," Haden said.

Areas without irrigation are *parched* and it is feared strong winds could cause dust storms that will increase the damage, he said.

The drought is expected to have a significant effect on world grain *stocks* and market prices. Although all consumers will suffer from the price hikes, hardest hit will be those in food-short countries dependent on American surplus grain to *stave off famine*.

Answer the following questions and then check the answers on page 173 in the answer key.
1. When did the drought begin?
2. What has the federal government done to help?
3. What is most needed now?
4. What problem would be caused by strong winds?
5. What effect will the drought in the United States have on other countries, particularly those that are short of food?

Crime and the Courts

 # Murder

JERSEY CITY, New Jersey, Nov. 10— *Alleged underworld* leader "Joey Boy" Galatro and three *bodyguards* were gunned down Thursday by unknown *assailants* after a brief gunbattle.

Galatro and two of the bodyguards died *instantly* in a hail of *bullets*, police said, while the third bodyguard remains in *critical condition* at Margaret Haig Hospital with *multiple* gunshot *wounds*.

One *eyewitness* told police the three or four *triggermen* were dressed in overalls and hard hats like construction laborers. One pulled a submachine gun from under a canvas wrap and sprayed the four with bullets, the witness said. The other gunmen reportedly fired handguns.

The *fusillade* of bullets immediately felled three of the men, but one of the bodyguards managed to pull his *pistol* and return the fire before being shot himself, witnesses said.

The gunmen then sprinted to a black automobile and roared off. Police said the getaway car was found *abandoned* just off Stegmen Parkway.

Police sources said the 48-year-old Galatro was the leader of an expanding new *crime syndicate challenging established* city *gangsters* for control of *protection rackets* and waterfront *theft*. They *theorized organized crime* leaders had *put out a contract* on Galatro to *eliminate* their *rival* and that professional killers were brought in from outside the state to do the job.

Another possible *motive* was *revenge* for last month's dockyard murder of a *suspected* gang member *brutally* beaten to death.

Galatro was *arrested* in connection with the *crime*, but *released* after eyewitnesses failed to *identify* him.

Two .38 caliber *automatics* were found at the scene and police said *ballistics tests* were being performed to see if either of them were the murder weapons.

Police are now waiting to question the *surviving* bodyguard when and if he *regains consciousness*.

Galatro had a long police record with his first arrest for *petty larceny* coming when he was 14 years old. He served a total of 17 years in prison on *convictions* ranging from illegal possession of weapons to armed robbery and *manslaughter*.

Try to answer the following questions as completely as possible and then check the answers on page 173 of the answer key.
1. Did Joey Boy Galatro kill anyone on Thursday?
2. Were the killers construction workers?
3. How many people were shot?
4. Was Galatro a criminal?
5. Galatro was arrested in connection with a murder the month before his death. Why was he set free?

Smuggling

LOS ANGELES, Nov. 11—Thai and American *narcotics officials* swooped down Friday on the storage center for a major international narcotics *network,* arresting eight persons and seizing more than 88 pounds of various *illegal* substances worth over $31 million on the *retail* market.

Police said they believed among the four Chinese, two Thais, and two Americans arrested is the *kingpin* of a *smuggling ring* capable of supplying the needs of about 10 percent of California's *heroin addicts.*

The *raid capped* an 18-month *investigation* by Thai narcotics *suppression* agents, the US Drug *Enforcement Administration* and the Los Angeles police department.

Tipped off by a police *informant* in Thailand, drug agents *traced* a shipment of teakwood furniture across the Pacific Ocean. *Customs* agents in San Francisco *verified* that the furniture *concealed* one of the largest single consignments of high-grade heroin ever to enter the United States from Southeast Asia, police said.

They said customs *authorities* then repacked the furniture and let it continue to its *destination* in a bay area *warehouse.*

Agents kept the shipment under *surveillance* for nearly two weeks before it was loaded on a truck and brought to Los Angeles.

Police said the furniture sat for another week in a shipping company before it was finally sent to a small house on Hernandez Avenue.

Armed with a *search warrant*, police and narcotics agents burst into the garage of the house as eight of the *accused* were testing the heroin for purity.

Identification of those arrested has been held up as police in Thailand are preparing to make further arrests in Bangkok and in the border area of northern Thailand known as the "Golden Triangle."

But police said one of those arrested was the head of a ring of California *drug pushers* that has been *peddling* nearly 10 percent of the state's heroin supply.

The heroin, packed in plastic tubes, was found in a secret compartment built into several chairs and in a false bottom of a desk. It amounted to 88 pounds worth $3 million *wholesale* and over $30 million retail in California.

In other places in the house, described as a narcotics storage center, agents found six pounds of *cocaine*, 22 pounds of *hashish*, and 50 pounds of *marijuana*. The entire *haul* was priced at $3.1 million wholesale, with a potential retail price of $31 million if sold on the street.

Answer these questions and check your answers against those on page 174 in the answer key.
1. Where were the drugs seized?
2. Where did the narcotics come from?
3. How much were the drugs worth wholesale?

4. Where were the drugs hidden?
5. Where were the narcotics first discovered?
6. How did the customs agents know the narcotics were hidden in the furniture?

③ Corruption

CLANSTON, Illinois, Jan. 25—City police Sunday *arrested* former Mayor Richard Weekly on a long list of *bribery, malfeasance, fraud, conspiracy*, and *corruption charges*.

Weekly, holding his *handcuffed* hands in front of his face, refused to speak to *reporters* as he was hauled into Weekly City Courthouse where he will be *indicted* later this week.

Ironically, the high-living Weekly will be held in the crumbling *cells* of the courthouse complex built during his last term which *allegedly* brought him more than $400,000 in *kickbacks* from construction companies.

The arrest came after a 19-month special *investigation* of numerous *irregularities* during Weekly's *administration*—called the most corrupt in American history.

Attorney for the investigating committee, Robert Renner, told newsmen the investigation has *unearthed evidence* of Weekly's *complicity* in *rackets bilking*

city, state, and federal governments of *vast sums*.

Renner said Weekly and *accomplices* who will be arrested shortly, made a *desperate* effort to *cover-up* the *scandal* with attempted bribery and *intimidation* of *law-enforcement officials*.

"Weekly regularly *abused his authority* to channel government *contracts* to his friends and secret business partners. He entered more than 50 *fictitious* names on city *payrolls* and simply collected their *salaries*," Renner said.

"Weekly bribed federal *bureaucrats* to overlook misuse of federal *funds* and a large portion of that money went to him and his *cohorts*," he said.

Renner charged Weekly and more than 40 other city officials were *guilty* of a wide range of *offenses* that *illicitly netted* them more than $150 million in his 16-year *reign* as mayor of the state's fourth largest city.

"He really was a king of corruption," Renner said.

Answer these questions and check your answers against those on page 174 in the answer key.
1. Was the present mayor of Clanston, Illinois, arrested?
2. Was Mr. Weekly charged with killing anyone?
3. Why is the jail he stayed in named Weekly Courthouse?
4. Whose money did Weekly take?
5. Were there any other corrupt officials?

④ Lawsuit

HOLLYWOOD, December 25—*Blue movie* starlet Lotta Love and her *financial* manager Thursday agreed to an out-of-court *settlement* ending a complex *legal wrangle* involving $50 million in *libel* and *breach of contract suits* over

the proceeds from Lotta's latest movie, "Deep Vee."

Attorneys for Miss Love and her manager, Nathan Bottomlyne, announced the two had reached an amica-

(Continued on next page)

(Continued from p. 110)
ble settlement with Bottomlyne paying an *undisclosed* amount of money to Miss Love in return for her agreement to allow the release of *assets frozen* by the court during the 27-month-long lawsuit.

Both sides have agreed to drop *charges* of *slander, defamation of character,* and breach of contract they had *filed* against each other, the lawyers said.

Bottomlyne also agreed to accept responsibility for tax *arrears* that piled up while the case was in court.

The settlement came after *Civil Court* Judge Anthony Nuse warned both *plaintiffs* of possible court action against them.

The bitter *dispute* began when Miss Love told reporters Bottomlyne *defrauded* her of most of the profit from her share of underground movie success "Deep Vee" which she starred in and co-produced with Bottomlyne.

Bottomlyne immediately filed suit for libel and slander, calling her a "sagging siren" who became successful only because of his direction.

Miss Love *counter-sued* for slander and breach of contract.

The two *complainants* made increasingly bitter charges against the other and then quickly filed new slander suits on the latest defamations.

After nearly a year of *litigation,* Miss Love filed for *bankruptcy claiming* the suit and Bottomlyne's failure to pay her had put her deeply in debt.

Miss Love's *creditors* joined the legal wrangle asking the court to *impound* all assets of Bottomlyne's "Top Notch" production company.

Lawyers said the final settlement included *compensation* to creditors but not enough to cover all court costs.

The lawyers said Miss Love and Bottomlyne have reached a *reconciliation* and are planning another co-production with Miss Love in the starring role in the near future.

Give full answers to these questions and then check them against those on page 174 of the answer key.

1. How much were the proceeds from Lotta's movie?
2. Did the judge make a decision in favor of Lotta?
3. Who is Nathan Bottomlyne?
4. Who was using the money while the case was in court?
5. What were Lotta and Bottomlyne fighting over?
6. Will they ever work together again?

 # Robbery

PARIS, Jan. 11—A *spectacular armored car* robbery last night ended in a wild gunbattle that left two *hold-up* men dead and a *hostage* seriously *wounded.*

Police have *launched* a *massive* manhunt to capture a third *bandit* believed to have escaped with over $1.3 million in cash, jewels, and *negotiable* securities.

The *drama* began when an armored car ferrying the contents of *safe deposit boxes* to the Banque de Lyons was struck by a large truck and sent slamming into a roadside ditch, police said.

Dazed by the crash, the bank guards were helpless when the robbers jumped out of the truck and tied them up. Police said the thieves used heavy *burglar* tools and explosives to break open the armored car.

A passing police patrol car turned to *investigate* the accident as the crooks were *rifling* the contents of the armored car. Police said the three robbers fled on foot across a nearby highway.

Commandeering a private car driven by a teen-aged girl, the three headed for (Continued on next page)

(Continued from p. 111)
central Paris with the patrol car in hot *pursuit*.

A plainclothes policeman spotted the car as it weaved through the back streets of the Latin Quarter. The plainclothesman tried to *apprehend* the *suspects*, *witnesses* said, but the thieves started shooting at him.

During the *commotion* the girl hostage tried to slip away from her captors, but just as she was crawling away from the car she was hit by a stray bullet, the witnesses said. Police said she was out of danger at Central Hospital.

The gunmen *abandoned* the car and holed up in a shop pouring fire on more than 50 policemen that *surrounded* their hideout, police said.

After making certain there were no *innocent bystanders* in the area, police *assaulted* the gunmen behind a barrage of *tear gas* and gunfire, a police spokesman said.

Police said they broke into the room, but found only two of the gunmen. Both men were seriously wounded when they were taken into custody and there was no sign of their *loot*.

One of the thieves, before lapsing into *unconsciousness*, said, "L'oiseau (the bird) *doublecrossed* us."

Police said the wounded gunman may have been referring to Henri D'aile, nicknamed "L'oiseau" and known throughout the underworld for his *incredible* escapes from the law.

Police *speculate* the third robber, whoever he was, escaped with the loot while his *accomplices* were fighting off the police.

D'aile was described as 5 feet 9 inches tall with a long thin nose and dark hair.

Answer the following questions and check your answers on page 174 of the answer key.
1. What was stolen?
2. How did the robbers break into the armored car?
3. How many people were shot?
4. How did the robbers stop the armored car?
5. Why didn't the guards on the armored car stop the robbers?
6. Was one of the robbers a teen-aged girl?
7. Who shot the girl?
8. How many robbers were there?
9. How many men were found when the police assaulted the robbers' hideout?

 6

Trial

PARIS, March 4—One of France's most *infamous underworld figures*, Henri "the Bird" D'aile yesterday *pleaded* not *guilty* to *charges* of *grand larceny, assault, kidnapping,* and murder *stemming from* a spectacular armored car robbery last January.

The *prosecutor*, however, told the court D'aile would be connected to the crime with *irrefutable evidence*.

"I am confident the court will find the *defendant* guilty as charged and end a *mockery of justice*," prosecutor Jean Cuneo said.

The dapper 36-year-old D'aile, who has been *accused* of numerous *crimes* in a 22-year crime career, but *convicted* of very few, said, "The case is based on *circumstantial evidence substantiated* only by the *testimony* of a dead man. The *allegations* are completely *unfounded*. The *judicial system* is simply trying to *revenge* itself for its previous failures to convict me," D'aile claimed.

D'aile was *arrested* in Le Havre several days after a *fatally wounded* robber *identified* him as an *accomplice* in an
(Continued on next page)

(Continued from p. 112)
armored car *heist* that *netted* him more than $1.7 million.

A charge of murder was added to the *indictment* when it was found that both robbers who died during the robbery were found to have been shot in the back with a .32 caliber pistol. No policemen at the scene were using a .32 caliber, said to be the favorite weapon of D'aile.

D'aile was first arrested and convicted for grand larceny in the robbery of a jewelry store when he was only 14. He was given a *suspended sentence.*

Two years later he was convicted in a *burglary* case and served six months in a boys' *reformatory* before escaping. Police didn't catch up with him for nearly three years when he was arrested in an elegant Paris apartment from which he ran a *lucrative embezzlement, blackmail,* and *extortion* ring employing *thugs* many years his senior.

D'aile studied law during his *imprisonment* and *appealing* his conviction got the *verdict overturned* on a *technicality.*

Since then D'aile has avoided conviction for anything more than *misdemeanors* and traffic *violations* despite being arrested 17 times and indicted five.

"The Bird is one of the *slickest operators* in the business," one Paris *detective* said, "but he won't be able to *clear* himself this time."

D'aile has been refused *bail* and the first hearing of the case is scheduled for next Wednesday.

Answer these questions trying not to look back at the story, then check the responses on page 174 in the answer key.
1. Did D'aile admit taking part in the robbery?
2. What happened to the two wounded robbers found by police the night of the robbery?
3. Why was D'aile charged with murder?
4. When was D'aile arrested for the first time?
5. When was he arrested most recently?
6. Is D'aile a lawyer?
7. Why do you think kidnapping was included in the charges?

Verdict

PARIS, May 22—Henri "the Bird" D'aile was *acquitted* today on *charges* that he *masterminded* a $1.7 million robbery last January, took a young woman *hostage*, and then shot his *accomplices* dead before getting away with the money.

Prosecutor Jean Cuneo *protested* the decision saying, "This is a travesty of justice. I intend to *file* an immediate *appeal*."

The criminal court *tribunal* ruled the *evidence* was *insufficient* to find D'aile guilty on *charges* of murder, *kidnapping*, or *grand larceny* among others.

D'aile, dressed in an elegant grey suit, told newsmen, "I was found *innocent* because I am innocent. It simply proves our *legal* system works."

He *accused* the police department of a personal *vendetta* against him. "I have been *arrested* six times in the past two years and never convicted. They just want to *harass* me," he *claimed*.

D'aile said the *verdict* would never be reversed on *appeal*.

The *turning point* in the *trial* came when key *witness*, Anne Jambaud, who had been taken hostage by the robbers, *admitted* under *cross-examination* that police had shown her a picture of D'aile and told her he was the third robber.

"Actually I never really saw the third man because he sat behind me," Miss Jambaud said.

The only other direct *evidence* tying D'aile to the *spectacular* armored car robbery was the whispered deathbed *confession* of one of the other two robbers.

"The Bird *doublecrossed* us," police *quoted* him as saying shortly before he died.

The .32 caliber weapon that killed the two thieves from behind as they waited for a police assault has never been found. Police were unable to locate the .32 caliber Berretta they said was D'aile's favorite weapon.

The *loot* from the robbert, $1.7 million in jewelry, cash, and *negotiable bonds* has not turned up.

"The *judgment* of the court *contradicts* the weight of the evidence," prosecutor Cuneo said, "and I intend to prove that in the Appeals Court."

Cuneo said he was considering bringing *perjury* charges against D'aile's mistress, Janine Lemontier, if the appeal is *sustained*.

Miss Lemontier gave D'aile an *alibi* police were unable to crack when she *testified* D'aile was in her apartment at the time of the robbery.

A final verdict is expected in three weeks.

Answer the following questions and then check page 174 in the answer key.
1. Was D'aile found guilty?
2. Will he go free now?
3. Why was D'aile acquitted?
4. Where did the police find the gun that killed the two thieves?
5. Where did D'aile's mistress say he was during the robbery?
6. Did the teen-aged hostage see D'aile during the robbery?

Business News

 # Budget

LONDON, June 14—The new Conservative Party government has proposed a tough *annual budget* designed to *spur* economic recovery with large *income tax* cuts and *tight monetary control.*

The *chancellor of the exchequer,* Sir Howard Geoffries, said cuts in personal income taxes would be balanced by increases in *sales taxes* and other indirect taxes.

He said, "A *tighter money supply* will help *curb inflation.*"

The government will depend on a *resurgence* in the *private sector* to lead the economic upturn, he said.

The budget provides for the sale of *nationalized industries* and sharp cuts in government spending to free *funds* for private *investment.*

The overall effect of the budgetary *measures* will be to "strengthen *incentives,* encourage the expansion of private industry, and reduce the government role in the economy," Sir Howard said.

The measures announced that the chancellor's budget message immediately *boosted* the *pound sterling* on world money markets against all other *currencies.*

But labor unions reacted *negatively* to the *proposals,* calling the budget "a prescription for wholesale *unemployment* and economic *recession.*"

Union leaders said they will seek minimum *wage settlements* of 20% because of expected cuts in *social services.*

Answer the following questions and check page 175 of the answer key.
1. Will income taxes rise or fall in Great Britain?
2. What will happen to other types of taxes?
3. What will be done to government spending if the budget is followed?
4. Will the government allow more or less money to circulate?
5. What was one immediate effect of the budget announcement?
6. Who did not like the budget? Why?

(2) Economic forecast

WASHINGTON, March 15—The *administration* of President Carl Arling today *predicted* another six months of slow *GNP* growth and rising *inflation*.

Chief economic advisor to the president, Walter Abel, told a news conference that increased foreign *competition*, rising prices for *raw materials*, and high *interest rates* would hold economic growth to less than 3% for the year with inflation rising above 7% for the first time in two years.

Abel said, however, that administration programs to restructure the economy would begin bearing fruit toward the end of the year and that growth in the gross national product would turn sharply upwards in the last *quarter*.

He said the administration would not allow the continued *sluggishness* of the economy to alter its free trade policies.

"Trade protectionism is an admission that US industry cannot compete," he said. "It avoids the real problem of how to upgrade our *industrial capacity* so it can win back the markets it has lost."

He said the administration of President Arling was determined to increase *investment* in *high technology* industries, upgrade aging plant equipment in heavy industry, and encourage workers to increase *productivity*.

Abel admitted that high interest rates threatened the *strategy*, but warned that any action to *artificially* lower interest rates *risked* fueling even greater inflation.

"We are still *recovering* from the recession caused by the previous administration and attempts to force the pace of recovery could be dangerous," he said.

Answer the following questions and then check page 175 in the answer key.
1. Is the forecast for the next six months good?
2. When will the economy start to grow at a faster rate?
3. Is Walter Abel the president?
4. What does the president plan to do to improve the economy?
5. Who did Abel blame for the slow growth of the economy?
6. Why does Abel think trade protectionism is not a good idea?

(3) Stocks

SINGAPORE, Feb. 16—Compu-Sing, Ltd., the four-year-old Singapore computer *manufacturing firm* has declared a record pre-tax *profit*, an increase in *dividends*, and a *free scrip issue*.

The firm, which *scored* heavily in the table-top business computer field, declared a pre-tax profit of over $14 million for 1981, up 43 percent over the previous year on *gross* sales of $92.3 million.

The company also announced a one for two *bonus issue* spurred by *share*

price increases of more than 150 percent over the past six months.

The share *split capitalizes* more than $8.2 million of *retained profit* and brings total paid up capital to $27.5 million.

Compu-Sing directors have declared a second *interim dividend* of 5 percent, less tax, bringing the total dividend so far this year to 15 percent.

Net profit after taxes is expected to be more than $11 million because of special Singapore tax *incentives* to high technology companies.

Answer the following questions and then check page 175 in the answer key.

1. Is Compu-Sing doing well?
2. Did the company make a net profit of $14 million in 1981?
3. Is the company issuing more stock? To whom?
4. After the issue, how many shares will a shareholder have if he started with 100 shares?
5. Will the company be paying money to its shareholders this year?
6. Can you figure out about how much tax the company expects to pay?

 # Stock market

NEW YORK, May 28–*Stock* prices closed higher in *moderate* trading yesterday after an early session *surge.*

A brief *bullish trend sparked* by *rumors* of a sharp drop in the money supply opened trading but the prices lost their *buoyancy* as *profit* takers became more active. Word circulated on the floor of the *exchange* at the opening that tomorrow's weekly money supply figures would show a large enough fall in the

(Continued on next page)

(Continued from p. 117)
money supply to allow the *Federal Reserve* to ease its *tight monetary policy*.

However, later information that the drop in the money supply would be insignificant hastened the *bearish* trend, but the selling pressure never grew strong enough to wipe out the early gains.

The *Dow Jones industrial average* bounced up to 984.30 up six points from the opening only to sag to 980.50, finishing 2.20 points up on the day.

Oil stocks led the early surge with Transcontinental Petroleum gaining 255 points to 1,134.

One top *broker* said he is advising his *clients* that the market is likely to remain steady over the next few months with no repetition of the dramatic price rises seen earlier in the year, after the election of President Carl Arling.

All the *leading indicators* show a period of stock market *stability* as the economic recovery of the past month gradually gains speed, the analyst said.

It is not a good time for *speculators*, but several brokers agreed that investors with well-chosen *portfolios* should *net* respectable earnings from growth expected to continue through at least the next two quarters.

Answer the following questions and then check page 175 in the answer key.
1. Did stock prices generally rise on May 28?
2. Did the prices rise most in the morning or afternoon?
3. Why did the price rise begin?
4. Why did it stop?
5. What is the major long-range prediction of some analysts?

Contracts

CLANSTON, Illinois, July 5—*Mayor* Richard Weekly today announced the award of construction *contracts* worth $9.5 million for the ultra-modern Weekly Courthouse Complex.

The contracts, which cover *excavation, piling, foundation* work, and structural steel supplies, were all sent to local Clanston construction companies.

"Our local boys may not have put in the lowest *tender bids*," Mayor Weekly said, "but we feel the local touch will bring a standard of quality to the work that those out-of-town companies can't match."

The largest contract, $3.2 million for foundation construction, went to the Ace Construction Company which has handled numerous city contracts before. Competing companies complained that the Ace tender was nearly $800,000 higher than the lowest bid.

Weekly said Ace's record of past cooperation with the city was what helped win them the contract.

The six contracts awarded today included heavy *penalty clauses* for failure to complete the work on schedule.

As compensation, Weekly said, the city has decided to *guarantee* bank *loans* to the construction companies so work can begin immediately.

The $19.8 million complex named in honor of the mayor is slated for completion in two years when Mayor Weekly completes his 25th year in office.

Answer the following questions and then check page 176 in the answer key.
1. What were the contracts awarded for?
2. Did the companies making the lowest bids for the work win the contracts?

3. What were two of the reasons the work was given to local companies, according to Mayor Weekly?
4. What happens if the work is not completed on schedule?
5. How is the city helping the construction companies?

Shipping

GENEVA, May 3—Developing countries have won important *concessions* that should increase their *share* of the world's shipping business.

At an international shipping conference just completed, 31 wealthy ship-owning countries have agreed to *ratify* a *treaty reserving cargoes* on regularly scheduled ocean liners to the two countries involved in the *transactions*.

The treaty was a response to what the developing countries complained were shipping *cartels* that *fixed freight rates* and divided the business of roughly 75% of the scheduled shipping lines.

The new treaty is designed to eliminate much of the influence of the cartels and give the developing countries more say in how rates are set as well as putting more cargoes in Third World ship bottoms.

The agreement is also expected to hurt the shipping companies operating their *fleets* under *flags of convenience* since the states registering the ships would have a very small percentage of the transactions. But observers noted that the treaty covers only cargoes going on regularly scheduled ocean liners, therefore leaving the vast majority of the shipping business unaffected.

Answer the following questions and then check page 176 in the answer key.
1. What is this story about?
2. What will the treaty do?
3. Who will the treaty help?
4. Who will the treaty hurt?

Foreign investment

TOKYO, July 21—The Japanese automotive industry announced today that it will substantially increase its *investments* in a variety of production projects in the United States.

The *pledge* came in response to increasing pressure from the US government and *appeals* from American labor unions.

Industry officials outlined the following projects expected to get underway next year:

—Donha Motors will begin construction on a $200 million *assembly plant* in Ohio for its popular line of economy cars.

—Lissan will establish a new *subsidiary* in Arkansas to produce its lightweight Satdun trucks.

—Wakasaki and Donha will expand existing motorcycle production *facilities* and enter *joint ventures* with local firms to produce motorcycle tires and brake assemblies.

(Continued on next page)

(Continued from p. 120)

—Yotata, the biggest Japanese manufacturer of automobiles, will launch a *feasibility study* for two major assembly plants and will enter *licensing* agreements and *joint stock enterprises* with American parts manufacturers to provide *spare parts* for imported models.

The measures are expected to ease criticism that the export sales of Japanese cars and trucks has hurt the US automotive industry, throwing hundreds of thousands of people out of work.

The total package of investment will eventually reach more than $250 million if all the projects *materialize.*

Answer the following questions and then check page 176 in the answer key.

1. Are US auto manufacturers increasing their investment in Japan?
2. Why is the Japanese auto industry investing in the United States?
3. Which company is studying whether to invest in production plants?
4. Which companies have definite plans to produce economy cars in the United States?
5. Which company wants American companies to make spare parts for its cars?
6. What do critics say is the effect of Japanese car exports?

 ## Trade balance

BONN, West Germany, May 11—West Germany's overall *balance of payments deficit* widened to $2.3 billion in April, up 24.5% from the same month last year, a finance ministry report said Monday.

Exports were up 17.2%, but *imports* rose even faster at 40.1% to $6.2 billion for the month.

Foreign aid and capital *lending* abroad increased the actual *currency* outflow to more than $7.6 billion versus an inflow of $55.3 billion.

Bank economists commented that the rising deficits were beginning to put inflationary pressure on the *deutschmark*

that should *counter* last year's deutschmark *appreciation* against the US dollar.

That increase in the value of the deutschmark, the economists said, was one reason for the new flood of *red ink* in the trade *statistics.* As the deutschmark became more highly valued, imports became cheaper and exports more difficult to sell.

Foreign exchange rate changes—not lowered *tariff barriers*—were the prime reasons for the increased imports that are expected to produce a $14.0 billion trade deficit for the year, the economists said.

Answer the following questions and then check page 176 in the answer key.

1. In April, did West Germany sell more or buy more from other countries?
2. Was the April deficit more than the preceding month?
3. Does West Germany lend money to foreign countries?

4. Did the deutschmark increase in value last year compared to other currencies?
5. How did the appreciation of the deutschmark affect the balance of trade?

⑨ Loan

AMSTERDAM, Aug. 5—A *consortium* of European banks has agreed to extend a federally *guaranteed loan* of $1.5 billion to Lord Motors, Inc. to keep the financially troubled American automobile manufacturer from sliding into *bankruptcy.*

The grouping of 36 European banks accepted conditions laid down by the US government for the guaranteed loan on easy interest loan terms.

Banking sources said much of the loan did not involve ready cash but came in the form of interest *concessions* and *deferrals* on some $900 million Lord already owed to the European banks.

A spokesman for Lord said the $1.5 billion would provide an adequate safety *margin* to keep the company out of bankruptcy, allow for unforeseen *contingencies*, and leave enough capital for investment in new plant equipment.

In Washington a spokesman for the Arling administration said the federal *guarantee* for the loan was not just to save the jobs of the 213,000 Lord employees, but to fulfill campaign pledges to get US industry back up to competitive levels with the latest machinery.

Answer the following questions and then check page 176 in the answer key.
1. Who is borrowing the money? Why?
2. Who is lending it?
3. Who is guaranteeing the loan? Why?
4. What is the amount of the loan? How much is in cash?

Strikes, Demonstrations, and Disputes

 # Strike

WASHINGTON, D.C.—More than 20,000 mineworkers *voted overwhelmingly* to accept the latest *contract* offered by mine *management* and end a 118-day coal mine strike that created a major *fuel* shortage.

Rank and file members gave their stamp of approval to a *package* of *benefits, pay hikes*, and safety *pledges submitted* by the leadership.

The agreement worked out with mineowners is the biggest contract ever won by the mineworkers, Union President Harold Baker said.

Spokesmen for employers said they viewed an agreement for *binding arbitration* after the first 30 days of a strike as a key step towards *moderation* and an end to *turmoil* in the mines.

With a vote of 13,734 to 6,890, mineworkers put an end to a *violence*-filled strike that brought production to a standstill and squeezed the nation's energy supplies.

The worst *incident* occurred only last week at Backbend Mines in West Virginia when, workers said, truckloads of *scabs*

and strike-breakers hired by the mineowner tried to drive past *picketlines*.

Armed guards opened fire from the trucks killing four picketers and wounding 17.

The *bloodshed spurred bargaining* efforts after three breakdowns of the talks, repeated *rejections* of contract offers, and walkouts by both sides.

In the final *session* a joint statement deplored the violence and presented a contract *proposal* that included salary *bonuses*, health benefits, and tough new *standards* for improved working conditions.

Baker said the two sides made the offer to *compromise* because "*strife* in the *pits* is not feeding our children or warming our homes."

The *negotiations* had come to the *brink* of a *settlement* before, but *activist* union members *opposed* the *deal* until last week's violence and the new contract offer.

Workers are expected to begin filing back into the mines tomorrow, but it will be at least next week before production resumes.

Answer the following questions and then check page 177 in the answer key.
1. Did the 20,000 mineworkers vote to go on strike?
2. What was one effect of the strike?
3. What did the workers get in the new contract?
4. What did the mineowners get in the new contract?
5. Were any workers killed in a violent incident at Backbend Mines?
6. When will the mines start producing coal again?

Wildcat strike

WAYNE, Michigan, Aug. 23—*Assembly line* workers at the 'Wayne auto *plant* staged an angry *wildcat strike* yesterday that led to *fistfights*.

Employees said the walkout began during the day *shift* shortly after a *foreman accused* line workers of *deliberately* stopping the line to rest.

Shop stewards from UCW (United Car Workers) *local* 219 *appealed* to workers to *resume* production after a two-hour *disruption*, but employees, *disgruntled* over steaming temperatures in the plant, *demanded* extra breaks when temperatures rose over 100 degrees.

Shouting matches between foremen and workers developed into brief fistfights. Management ordered the shift to leave work early to prevent the *chaotic* conditions in the plant from leading to *damage* to equipment.

Union officials said the problem was an ordinary *dispute* over proper working conditions and could be handled through regular *grievance procedures*.

Defiance of the rules, one official said, might weaken the union position at upcoming contract *negotiations*.

"We must show some union *discipline* if we are to get our demands," he said.

Militant workers, however, *threatened* to *paralyze* production with repeated stoppages until the complaints were acted upon.

Answer the following questions and then check page 177 in the answer key.
1. Who went out on strike?
2. Was the strike carefully planned?
3. Why was there a strike?
4. Did the union order the strike?
5. How many conflicting groups are there and who are they?

Slowdown

ROME, Jan, 23—*Discontented* railway workers yesterday began a slowdown that *sparked* nationwide *disruption* of train services in an effort to *overturn* new *curbs* on *featherbedding*.

Delays up to 13 hours *stemming from* the *job action* were reported on the Rome-Milan line with lesser delays on every line.

Union members started a "*work-to-rule*" after last minute efforts to avert the

(Continued on next page)

(Continued from p. 123)
go-slow fell through during a stormy negotiating session in which union representatives *rejected proposals* by a government *mediator*.

"We apologize for any inconvenience to passengers caused by this dispute, but I must *emphasize* that we are acting with *moderation* and have stopped short of a strike," union secretary general Joseph Pessarella said.

"If they want to cut down our *crews*, the men will have to be more careful and *abide* by all the rules—this is why your trains are late," he said.

Railroad *officials* said they were simply trying to reduce the number of men aboard the trains in order to provide cheaper, more *efficient* service to the public.

"We have to *challenge* the unions or they will *bog down* the railroads with still more useless men," one official said.

Answer the following questions and then check page 177 in the answer key.
1. Did the railway workers in Italy go on strike?
2. What disrupted train service?
3. What are railroad officials trying to accomplish with the curbs on featherbedding?
4. Why are the railway workers unhappy with the restrictions?

④ Protest demonstration

HUNTSBURY, Aug. 11—Police fired *tear gas* and *arrested* more than 5,000 *passively resisting protestors* Friday in an attempt to break up the largest anti-nuclear *demonstration* ever staged in the United States.

More than 135,000 demonstrators *confronted* police on the construction

site of a 1,000-megawatt nuclear power plant scheduled to provide power to most of southern New Hampshire.

Organizers of the huge demonstration said that the protest was continuing despite the police actions. More demonstrators were arriving to keep up the (Continued on next page)

(Continued from p. 124)
pressure on state *authorities* to *cancel* the project, they said.

The demonstrators have *charged* that the project is unsafe in the *densely* populated area, would create *thermal pollution* in the bay, and had no acceptable means for *disposing* of its *radioactive* wastes.

"The demonstrations will go on until the jails and the courts are so overloaded (with arrested demonstrators) that the state judicial system will collapse," one organizer said.

Governor Stanforth Thumper insisted there would be no reconsideration of the power project and no delay in its construction set for completion in three years.

"This project will begin on time and the people of this state will begin to receive its *benefits* on schedule. Those who break the law in *misguided* attempts to *sabotage* the project will be dealt with according to the law," he said.

Police said *reinforcements* were being called in from all over the state to handle the disturbances.

The protests began before dawn Friday when several thousand demonstrators broke through police lines around the *cordoned-off* construction site.

The demonstrators *defied* police orders to move from the area. Tear gas cannisters fired by police failed to *dislodge* the protestors who had come prepared with their own *gas masks* or facecloths.

Finally gas-masked and *helmeted* police charged into the crowd to drag off the demonstrators one by one. The protestors did not resist police, but refused to walk away under their own power.

Those arrested will be charged with unlawful *assembly, trespassing*, and disturbing the peace, police said.

The protestors carried *placards* that read "No Nukes is Good Nukes," "Sunpower, Not Nuclear Power," and "Stop Private Profits from Public Peril."

Answer the following questions and then check page 177 in the answer key.

1. What are the demonstrators protesting about?
2. Did the police end the demonstration?
3. How many demonstrators were there?
4. Who fired tear gas?
5. Who had gas masks?
6. Did the demonstrators fight the police?
7. How do the leaders of the demonstrators think the arrest of so many people will help their protest?

War and Terrorism

① Invasion

BAGHDAD, Iraq, Dec. 1—Iraqi *troops* led by *tanks* and *backed* by long-range *artillery* yesterday *launched* their second major *invasion* of Iran.

Iraqi national television said the thrust across the border was "to *liberate* our *oppressed* Arab *brethren* in the west of Iran" and to defend Islam "against the *distortion* and *destruction* taught by the false *prophets*" in Tehran.

Taking advantage of the political
(Continued on next page)

(Continued from p. 126)
turmoil in Iran, the well-equipped Iraqi forces broke through Iranian *defenses* at two points, *intelligence analysts* said.

Two separate *armored columns* successfully *bridged* the *strategic* Shatt-al-Arab waterway and *advanced* toward the cities of Korramshahr and Abadan, only recently rebuilt after destruction in the 1980–83 Iran-Iraq war.

Counterattacks by the brave, but poorly armed and led, Iranians failed to slow the advance of the motorized columns sporting the latest Soviet weaponry.

Weakened by *assassination* and civil *strife* following the death of the *revered* Iranian religious leader last year, Iran's armed forces appeared ill-prepared for the attack.

Artillery *barrages battered* the frontline defenses left undermanned by the reassignment of *crack* troops to *suppress rioting* in the capital last month.

There were no immediate *estimates* of *casualties* except an Iranian news agency report that said the defenders were "holding out bravely despite heavy *casualties*."

Analysts said Iraq's invasion force of 17 *divisions* totaling nearly 150,000 men faced only about 80,000 defenders.

Three *squadrons* of Iraqi fighter bombers, mostly Soviet-built MiGs, appeared to control the air against the small numbers of aging American F-4 Phantom jets the Iranian air force was able to send against them.

After *initial dogfights* with the outnumbered Iranian planes, the Iraqi air force *concentrated* on *tactical* bombing and *strafing* attacks on Iranian positions.

Military experts said there was no hope of saving the two Iranian cities from capture unless the Iranian military *command*, hard hit by political *purges*, could *mobilize* the strategic *reserves* and bring them to the *battlefront* within five days.

Answer the following questions and then check page 178 in the answer key.

1. Which army has crossed the border into what country's territory?
2. Why are the Iranian forces weak?
3. What weapons are the invading forces using?
4. Who is winning the air war? Why?
5. What has happened to the Iranian military command?
6. How many times has Iraq invaded Iran?

(2) # Guerrilla attack

IRALA, Paraguay, June 24—More than 200 heavily armed Communist *guerrillas raided* a police post in western Paraguay in a pre-*dawn* attack yesterday that left at least 15 people dead on both sides, police reports said.

Police officials in Irala district, 150 miles west of Asuncion, the capital, said the *insurgents* poured rocket and machine-gun fire into the district police station for more than three hours before *reinforcements* arrived to drive them off.

Twenty-six police and *volunteer* defenders put up *stiff resistance*, but several outlying buildings were overrun by the *terrorists* who seized 24 assault rifles and 60 boxes of *ammunition*.

After losing six men killed in the first moments of the firefight, the police *commander* called for help.

An army *base* three miles away sent a *relief column* that immediately ran into an *ambush*.

(Continued on next page)

(Continued from p. 127)
The soldiers, with three *armored personnel carriers* and an *armored car*, pushed through the ambush without *casualties* when a *landmine* planted by the Communists failed to explode, the report said.

The guerrilla force attacking the police station *retreated* hastily with the arrival of the reinforcements.

A helicopter gunship *strafed* the retreating guerrilla band as it plunged through the heavy jungle surrounding the police station.

Military authorities ordered an all-out *pursuit* of the terrorists before they could reach their mountain *stronghold* just across the border with neighboring Argentina.

A government spokesman said the Communist *tactics* indicated growing *desperation*.

"Our counter-insurgency techniques have effectively *isolated* the terrorists from their *sources* of supply both in the villages and from abroad," the spokesman said.

He said government *operations* in the past few weeks had captured seven guerrilla arms *caches* in the rugged mountains around Irala. "It is clear that the latest attack was an attempt to *recoup* their losses at a *single stroke*," he said.

Answer the following questions and then check page 178 in the answer key.

1. Did the Communist guerrillas attack a police post in western Paraguay?
2. Why did the guerrillas raid the police post, according to the government?
3. What did the guerrillas take?
4. What happened to the soldiers coming to help the police?
5. Were any soldiers in the armored personnel carriers killed?
6. Where did the guerrillas have their camp?
7. What did the government soldiers do when the guerrillas retreated?

③ Refugees

KHAO I DANG, Thailand, June 9— More than 80,000 *refugees* have signed up for *repatriation* to Cambodia since last month's *ceasefire* and agreement on a *neutral* government.

But another 1,200 refugees still want *resettlement* in the west.

A representative of the United Nations High Commissioner for Refugees said arrangements were already being made for the return of the refugees to their homes in time for next month's U.N. supervised elections.

The refugees were the remainder of the nearly 250,000 Cambodians who fled nearly 18 years of war and *starvation* in their homeland.

After taking first *asylum* in Thailand, more than 100,000 Cambodians were *resettled* in third countries.

But many were never *classified* as refugees. To discourage the outflow many were called *illegal immigrants* and forbidden the chance of resettlement. They were kept in sprawling camps near the border waiting for the *negotiated* settlement that finally came last month.

With U.N. troops gradually *disarming* the three *mutually antagonistic* Cambodian *factions*, most of those in the camps said they thought it was now safe to go home.

Most will be sent by bus across the
(Continued on next page)

(Continued from p. 128)
border and given sufficient food and supplies to reach their home villages.

But another 1,200 refugees still seek resettlement.

"Who knows how long the peace will last," said one of those refusing to go. "I don't want us to become refugees once again."

Thai officials said it was up to the western governments to decide what to do with the last refugee remnants.

"Our policy is that they must all leave Thailand by the end of the month," one official said. "If they are not resettled abroad, then they must be repatriated, forcibly if necessary."

Answer the following questions and then check page 178 in the answer key.

1. Where are the refugees from?
2. Where are most of them going?
3. Why did they flee to Thailand?
4. Why are they returning home?
5. Do some refugees fear to go home?
6. Who is making arrangements for the return of the refugees?
7. How many refugees were able to resettle in new homes in third countries?

Nuclear arms race

WASHINGTON, May 7—The Soviet Union's *parity* in *nuclear weapons* will enable it to use its *superiority* in *conventional weapons* to win any future *confrontation* with the west in Europe, according to a *Pentagon* report *issued* today.

The study, ordered by the *Defense Department, recommended* that current *strategic weapons* be *adapted* to a *tactical role* and that both development and *deployment* be *boosted* for conventional weapons. With strategic weapons *arsenals* of both the United States and the Soviet Union capable of *decimating* each other's population and *demolishing* all major cities, the study said the most important arms race is in conventional weaponry—making the foot, air, and tank soldier even more *lethal*.

It has recommended the *urgent* development of a lightweight *missile*, capable of being carried by a single soldier, but able to *blast* through the heavy *armor* of the latest Soviet *tanks*.

"The present *cruise missile* should be *refined* and adapted to battlefield use against *massed armor* at long range," the study said.

A complete revision of *mobilization* plans was called for along with beefed-up regular forces and an increased number of troops on regular *alert*.

"Under present *regulations* it would be more than six months before even the *active reserves* could be fully mobilized to fight abroad," the study said.

In side notes to the main proposals, a rapid *expansion* of the killer submarine force and the *fighter-interceptor* force in Asia was suggested to prevent a *blockade* of Japan.

"Unless conventional armed forces are given a major *overhaul*, parity in nuclear weapons will be worthless, because disadvantages in conventional weaponry and readiness mean that *threats* will leave us only the alternatives of nuclear *annihilation* or *appeasement*," the study concluded.

Answer the following questions and then check page 178 in the answer key.

1. Does the Soviet Union have superiority in atomic weapons over the United States according to a Pentagon report?
2. Does the Soviet Union have more and more powerful non-atomic weapons than the US?
3. According to the report, who would win a conventional war in Europe?
4. What is the most important arms race now, according to the report?
5. What target does the report want the cruise missile adapted to hit?
6. What kind of missile did the report recommend be developed?
7. What is wrong with mobilization plans for US reserves?
8. What do you think was the most important general conclusion of the report?

 # Hijack

HEATHROW, England, Nov. 12— *Commandos* in *disguise rescued* unharmed 130 passengers from a *hijacked* airliner after 17 hours of *terror* in a *lightning raid* that killed two *radicals* as they were about to *execute* their *hostages.*

Security officials said they were forced to take *violent* action because they were convinced the two *terrorists* of the Force for *Liberation* of *Oppressed* People (F.L.O.P) were going to *carry out* their *threat* to shoot one passenger every five minutes until the government *gave in* to demands to *release* all "political prisoners."

Passengers said the *ordeal* began when two young men sprang from their seats waving machine *pistols* and handgrenades while the plane was mid-Atlantic.

Pilot Robert Aston said one of the men forced his way into the *cockpit* threatening to blow up the plane unless he was allowed to radio his *demands.*

Police said the still *unidentified* terrorist demanded the release of all political prisoners. He insisted that they be taken to the airport and exchanged for the passengers.

After landing at the airport, government *negotiators* spoke to the terrorists in a 15-hour effort to persuade the radicals that their demands were being met,

but that women and children must be released first.

All approaches to the airport were *sealed off* and armed guards were *posted.* Police *marksmen* were *stationed* on the roofs of the airport and hidden behind equipment near the plane.

Passengers said except for the first few minutes when several people cried hysterically, there was no *panic.* They said the hijackers used the time to try to *indoctrinate* their hostages aboard the plane to the *cruelty* and *injustice* of the world political and economic system.

But late into the night the terrorists ran out of patience and set a *deadline.*

"If the political prisoners are not out on the runway by midnight," the terrorist leader said, "we will begin to *execute revolutionary justice* on the *bourgeois capitalist* prisoners of the F.L.O.P.

"Any attempt to use force will be *futile* and result in a *massacre.* If we cannot save the lives of those *victims* of state *repression,* we can at least *avenge* them," the terrorist *commander* said.

"We can have no *mercy* because the system of *exploitation* we are fighting to *overthrow* is merciless. Long live the revolution!"

More than 130 men and women dressed in prison clothing were brought
(Continued on next page)

130

(Continued from p. 130)
out on the runway just as the terrorists brought the first passenger to the door of the plane with a pistol pointed at his head.

But as the hijackers smiled and waved to approaching "prisoners," they were cut down by *sniper* fire from the *terminal*. The "prisoners," commandos and police- women in disguise, *hurled concussion grenades* into the open door of the plane, pulled out their weapons, and *charged* forward.

The nonlethal grenades *stunned* the *wounded* terrorists with blasts and light so they were unable to *explode* their grenades before bullets from the commandos slammed into them, killing both.

Answer the following questions and then check page 179 in the answer key.

1. How many passengers were killed on the hijacked airliner?
2. Who was killed?
3. Why did security officials order the commando attack on the hijackers?
4. What did the hijackers want?
5. Did the government release any prisoners?
6. How did the commandos get near the plane?

Energy

 # Oil

WASHINGTON, April 7—US President Carl Arling *bluntly* told the American people yesterday they must begin to use less energy and pay more for it.

Warning "our national strength is again becoming dangerously dependent on a thin line of oil tankers," Arling said he will begin taking price controls off *domestically* produced *crude* oil in June.

The *multi-phase* de-control *scheme* is expected to add four or five cents to the price of a gallon of gasoline, diesel fuel, and heating oil.

Arling said the higher prices will encourage both conservation and exploration—thus reducing the country's dependence on supplies from OPEC (Organization of Petroleum Exporting Countries).

At the same time, the President said, a "windfall *profits* tax" would *divert* some of the expected $16 billion increase in oil *revenues* from oil companies to the *federal* government.

"Windfall profits," Arling explained, would include all extra revenues *generated* solely by the sudden jump in prices.

Arling said the money would be used to *finance mass transit*, help the poor *cope* with higher energy costs and develop *alternative energy sources*.

He warned that failure to act immediately could result in widespread *shortages* this winter. He said he would request *standby* powers to *ration* gasoline and heating oil if the supply situation *deteriorated* more quickly than expected.

Answer the following questions and then check page 179 in the answer key.
1. What will happen to the price of oil and oil products?
2. Why did President Arling announce the measures?
3. What will he do about the extra profits oil companies make from the increased price of their products?
4. What will he do with the extra money from taxes?
5. What did he warn might happen if oil was not conserved?

② Nuclear power

WASHINGTON, April 3—The recent breakdown of the Oyster Bay nuclear *power* plant has not only threatened the lives of hundreds of thousands of people, but also the future of nuclear power in an energy-short world.

Although experts still argue over the long-term effects of *radiation contamination* that *leaked* from the crippled *generating* plant, no one *disputes* that the *prospects* for *widespread* use of atomic power have been seriously hurt—at least for a while.

The closure of nuclear plants for safety reasons has already cost the United States thousands of *megawatts* in generating capacity and increased the danger of electrical *blackouts* throughout the country.

Rising fears about the safety of *reactors* have also *complicated* the government's attempts to *alleviate* the current oil shortage.

The fears go beyond a failure of cooling systems as happened at Three Mile Island and even beyond a *core meltdown* and resulting widespread release of radioactivity.

The faith of the public in technological answers to the safety problem has been severely shaken, but most scientists still point to the fact that commercial nuclear power has not caused a single *fatality*.

But the problem of nuclear waste *disposal*, even *ardent proponents* of nuclear power admit, is still far from satisfactorily solved.

The progress of *commercial* atomic power may be brought to an *abrupt halt* if *critics* can push through Congress a *bill* banning new *licenses* for nuclear plants until scientists discover a safe way to *dispose permanently* of radioactive waste.

Answer the following questions and then check page 179 in the answer key.
1. What broke down?
2. What was threatened by the breakdown?
3. Have any nuclear power plants been closed for safety reasons?
4. What seems to be the most difficult problem concerning nuclear plants?
5. What may be one result of the closed nuclear plants?

③ # The future

ROME, Dec. 17—A new computer-aided report from the conservationist Earth Club indicates that without major *policy* changes a severe *shortage* of oil by the year 2000 will force a *drastic* fall in production, *widespread unemployment, soaring inflation*, and *choking pollution*.

The report, based on a computer model assuming present patterns of industrial growth, said by the end of the century petroleum will provide only one-third of the world's energy needs.

Natural gas production will fall off even more sharply, it said, and most of the world's gas and oil pipelines and *refineries* will be working at less than 35 percent *capacity*—further reducing *efficiency* and increasing waste.

Soaring prices will encourage *exploitation* of difficult-to-extract oil and gas deposits, it said. Even assuming double current world estimated reserves, the computer predicted supplies would not come close to meeting world needs.

The report said a large increase in the use of coal was the only short-run possibility. But it warned massive use of coal—both clean-burning anthracite and more plentiful, but more polluting, lignite—would sharply increase worldwide air pollution with *unforeseeable* effects on *climate* and world oxygen levels.

The report was nearly as *pessimistic* about more *exotic* energy sources.

Solar power, it said, would provide much needed energy inputs, especially for home heating, but was too limited— at least with present technology—for the major power requirements of industry, transportation, and electrical *generation*.

Wind, *geothermal*, and *hydroelectric* power were also useful, the report said, but too limited to have much effect on total energy supplies.

The report indicated questions of safety, *radioactive* waste *disposal*, and limited supplies of *enriched* uranium would severely *retard* the growth of nuclear *fission* power.

It predicted the *breeder-reactor*, so called because it produces ("breeds") more fuel than it consumes, could only come into use when worries about its end product—dangerous, *weapons-grade* plutonium—could be put to rest. It said the breeder reactor, whose development has been halted in the United States for safety reasons, could not possibly be on line before the year 2000 and the predicted energy *crunch*.

The last alternative examined was that of *fusion* power.

The study concluded that even with the best of luck and *massive* government spending, fusion would only just be coming into use as the *crisis* hit—too little and too late to help.

The report concluded there was no single answer to the energy crisis. It suggested that a drastically revised "world energy life style" that included much less industrial growth, *vigorous* energy *conservation* schemes, lower population growth, and much higher use of *replenishable* energy sources—such as solar power—was the only way to soften, if not avoid, the worst effects of the coming energy shortage.

Answer the following questions and then check page 179 in the answer key.

1. Does the report indicate a good future ahead?
2. Will there definitely be a drastic fall in production in the year 2000?
3. What is the major cause of the problems the report says are likely?
4. What is the problem with using more coal as a substitute for oil?
5. Can solar power fill the need?
6. What is wrong with using the breeder-reactor?
7. Is there a single answer to the energy shortage problem?
8. What were the assumptions of the computer model used in the report?

Glossary

abandon—to leave completely with no intention of using again; to stop

abide—to follow

abortion—the act of causing a baby to be born too early for it to live

abrupt—sudden

abuse authority—to use power improperly

accelerate—to increase speed

access—the ability to use

accomplice—a partner in crime

accord—a formal agreement between two or more countries

accuse—to claim that someone has done something wrong

acquit—to determine to be not guilty

active reserve—that part of the armed forces which is kept in frequent training, ready to be used in case of a war, but still not part of the regular army

activist—a person who favors extreme action

adapt—to change in some way to make suitable

addict—a person who has developed a physical need for something, especially a drug

administration—the persons managing a government at a particular time

admit—to say to be true

advance—to move forward

agenda—a list of subjects to be discussed

aggression—the wrongful attempt to take over territory belonging to another country

agriculture—concerning farming

aid—1. to support; help   2. support; help

aide—a helper; an assistant

ail—to trouble

ailing—in poor condition; weak

aim—to point in a particular direction

alarm—a warning signal or sound

alert—readiness for action

alibi—a claim by an accused person that he was not present at the time a crime happened

allegation—an accusation

allege—to claim to be true

allegedly—it is claimed

alleviate—to make less

alliance—an agreement between two or more countries, especially for military cooperation

allied—united militarily

allotment—money that has been set aside for a particular purpose

alternative—a choice

alternative energy source—a type of energy not now commonly in use

ambush—an attack from a hidden position

amendment—a change in a law or a proposed law

ammunition—material, such as bullets and gunpowder, used in the firing of a weapon

amphibious—capable of working on land or in the sea

analyst—a person who studies a situation carefully

annihilation—complete destruction

annual—happening every year

anonymous—unnamed; unidentified

antagonism—active opposition

appeal—1. to ask for help   2. a request for a higher court to reconsider the decision of a lower court   3. popularity

appeasement—the giving in to the demands of a country that threatens to use force

appoint—to give a function or position to

appreciation—a rise in value

apprehend—to take into control; to arrest

arbitration—the hearing and deciding of a disagreement by a person acceptable to both sides

archfoe—chief enemy

ardent—having strong feelings about something

arid—very dry

arm—to supply with a weapon

arm twisting—persuasion

armed—carrying a weapon

armor—a covering of strong metal for protection

armored car—a vehicle protected with a covering of strong metal

armored personnel carrier—a protected vehicle for carrying soldiers

arrears—the state of being behind in payments

arrest—to seize a person under the power of the law

arsenal—total supply of weapons and military equipment

articulate—skilled in speech

artificial—1. man-made; not real   2. done in an unnatural way

artillery—guns raised on supports

ash—the powdery remains of something that has been burnt

assailant—a person who attacks another person

assassination—a planned killing of a person

assault—to attack with violence

assembly—a gathering together

assembly line—an arrangement of men and machines in a factory for the putting together of a product

assembly plant—a building where the various parts of a product are put together

asset—something of value

asylum—the right to stay in another country after one has left one's own country for political reasons

attorney—a lawyer

authorize—to allow or give the power to do

authority—a person who has the power to control or command

automatic—a kind of gun that can fire quickly and repeatedly

avenge—to give satisfaction for a wrong received by causing harm to the guilty person or group

avert—to avoid

back—to support

bail—release from prison in return for money or property given to make certain the person will return at a given time

balance of payments—the difference between the exports and the imports of a country

ballistics test—a test to determine whether a particular bullet was fired from a particular gun

ballot—1. one round of voting   2. the total number of votes   3. a piece of paper used in voting

bandit—a robber, especially one who uses force

bankruptcy—the condition of being unable to repay what one owes

banner—a flag or sign

banquet—a large formal dinner

bargaining—an attempt at coming to an agreement by considering suggestions made by both sides

barrage—heavy gunfire

barrier—something placed in order to block or control people or things, especially to prevent from entering an area

base—a protected area from which an army works

batter—to hit repeatedly and cause heavy damage

battle—a struggle or fight

battlefront—the place of fighting

bearish—stock prices tending to fall

benefit—1. a payment or other help given by an organization 2. something good

bid—to offer a price in trying to win a contract

bilk—to cheat, especially out of money

bill—a plan for a law

binding arbitration—the settlement of a disagreement by which the disagreeing sides promise to follow the decision of a person approved by both sides

blackmail—demanding money in return for not telling harmful information

blackout—a loss of electrical power

blast—1. an explosion 2. to explode

blaze—a fire

blockade—the shutting off of a place, preventing movement in or out

bloodshed—violence causing injury or death

blue movie—a movie that contains much realistic sex

bluntly—directly without attempting to soften

bodyguard—a person who is hired to protect another person from harm

bog down—to cause to function slowly and poorly

bond—a paper indicating ownership of a debt due from a government or business organization, usually giving the owner a fixed rate of interest

bonus—something given or paid above what is necessary

bonus issue—the issue of stock certificates in addition to dividends paid, usually after a very profitable year

boost—to increase; to cause to rise

border—the dividing line between two areas

bottle up—to shut in

bourgeois—a member of the middle class; a person owning property

breach of contract—the breaking of a legal agreement

breeder-reactor—a nuclear reactor that produces more fuel than it uses

brethren—members of the same group

bribery—something given or promised to a government official in return for favored treatment

bridge—to cross by means of a bridge

brink—edge

broker—an agent who buys and sells stock for other people

brutal—very cruel

budget—a plan for spending money

bullet—a small metal ball that is fired from a gun

bullish—stock prices tending to rise

buoyancy—upward movement

bureaucrat—a person who works for a government department

burglar—a person who breaks into and enters a building, usually in order to steal something

cabinet—a group of leaders who manage the government of a country

cache—a place where something is kept hidden

calibre—a measure of the distance across the hole of a gun

campaign—1. the period before an election during which candidates attempt to persuade voters to vote for them   2. to attempt to persuade voters to vote in a particular way

cancel—to stop

cancer—a serious illness involving abnormal growth in the body

candidate—a person who is attempting to win an election or a position

cap—to complete

capacity—the total amount able to be produced

capital—money

capitalist—a person who has put money into private business

capitalize—the provision of money for a company to use to buy equipment, plant, or property when it gets started

capsize—to turn over

cardinal—a high-ranking Catholic priest who is a member of the group that chooses the church's leader

cargo—goods carried by a ship

carnage—the killing or injuring of large numbers of people

carry out—to do an action that has been planned

cartel—an international group formed to control output and prices in some field of business

casualty—killed or injured person

catastrophe—a disaster

caucus—a meeting of local members of a political party

ceasefire—an agreement to stop fighting

cell—a room for a prisoner

challenge—1. to dare   2. to compete with   3. to refuse to yield to   4. a problem requiring great skill to solve

chancellor of the exchequer—(in the British Government)—the minister in charge of finances

chaotic—very confused and disorganized

charge—1. to say that something is wrong; to accuse of wrongdoing   2. a written statement saying that something has been done which is against the law

charismatic—having qualities that give a person powerful influence over other people

charred—burnt to a black color

choke—to prevent from breathing

circumstantial evidence—indirect evidence; evidence that tends to prove a fact by proving that a situation existed that makes the fact in question reasonably certain

civil court—a court that decides noncriminal cases, such as lawsuits

civil strife—trouble among two or more groups within a country

claim—a demand for something one feels one has a right to

clause—a part of a contract

clear—to prove to be innocent

clemency—mercy; a lessening of a punishment

client—a customer who pays someone to perform a service

climate—the weather conditions of a region

clinic—a place for the treatment of ill or injured people who do not need to stay in a hospital

coalition—a combination of groups

coast—the edge of land next to the ocean

cocaine—an illegal drug taken from coca leaves

cockpit—the place in the front of an airplane where pilots sit

cohort—partner, especially in wrongdoing

collapse—a complete breakdown

collective—of a group of individuals working together

collide—to crush; to hit together with force

colonial—concerning land owned and ruled by another country

column—a long line of soldiers and their equipment

comb—to search very carefully

command—leadership

commandeer—to take by force

commander—a military or police leader; a leader who has the power to give orders

commando—an armed force with special training, able to carry out difficult and dangerous actions

commercial—prepared for sale; for business purposes

commission—1. a group of people with the power to perform a certain function   2. to place an order for a piece of work

commitment—support

commotion—confused and often violent activity

communique—an official statement given to the press or public

compensation—1. payment   2. something given in return

competition—1. a struggle between two or more people, groups, or organizations to gain something   2. a struggle between two or more economic organizations to win customers

competitiveness—the ability to compete

complainant—a person who brings a complaint to a court of law

complicate—to make difficult

complicity—involvement in wrongdoing

component—a part of something

comprehensive—thorough and complete

compromise—to settle a disagreement by accepting less than one's goal on the condition that the other side does so too

conceal—to hide

concentrate—to give special attention to

concentration camp—a prison camp for political prisoners

concession—something that has been yielded or given up

conciliatory—trying to overcome a distrust or dislike

concussion grenade—a small bomb that disables a person for a short time but does not kill

condemn—to express strong disapproval or dissatisfaction with

conference—a meeting

confession—an admission of guilt

confirm—to make certain or sure

confront—to face in opposition

confrontation—war; a disagreement between two or more sides that may lead to war

consciousness—the condition of being awake and aware of one's surroundings

consensus—a general agreement

conservation—the act of saving something from overuse

conservative—a person who is generally against major changes in the political system and opposed to a large government role in society

consolidate—to strengthen

consortium—a group that comes together to provide a very large amount of money for a business activity

consumption—the buying of goods or services

contamination—the making of something impure or unhealthy

contingency—a possible occurrence

contract—a legal agreement

contradict—to show the opposite of what has been stated

controversial—causing disagreement

convention—a meeting of a political party in which candidates are chosen and policy is made

conventional weapon—a nonnuclear weapon

convict—1. to prove or decide that a person is guilty   2. a person who has gone to prison for doing something against the law

conviction—a court decision that a person has done something against the law

cope—to deal with successfully

cordon off—to close off an area and prevent people from entering

core meltdown—the overheating of the radioactive core in a nuclear reactor, releasing dangerous radiation

correspond—to be connected in some way

corruption—dishonesty, especially on the part of a government official

council—a group of people selected to work together as a unit

counter—to work against

counter-sue—to sue someone who has already sued you

counterattack—an attack against an enemy who has attacked previously

counterpart—a person who does the same job as another

court—a place where cases of law are heard and decided

cover up—to try to prevent the true facts from being known

crack—well trained and highly skilled

creditor—a person to whom money is owed

crew—1. the group of people who work on an airplane or ship   2. a group of people who do a particular kind of work

crime—an unlawful act that is cause for punishment

crime syndicate—an organization of criminals and their businesses

criminal court—a court that hears and decides cases that involve crimes

crisis—a very important and serious time; a decisive moment

critic—a person who points out faults in something

critical condition—in danger of dying

crop—the fruit or grain grown by a farmer

cross examination—(in a court)—the questioning of a person who supports the opposite side, in an attempt to disprove what has been said

crude—raw or unprepared

cruel—causing great pain or discomfort; very unkind

cruise missile—a missile that carries a powerful and sometimes nuclear explosive, guided by sophisticated electronic gear. Unlike other missiles, it flies at low altitudes and at a relatively slow speed. It is extremely difficult to detect.

crumpled—bent and pressed out of normal shape

crunch—a shortage

crux—the most important point

culmination—the high point

curb—1. to reduce or stop   2. a control

cure—something that restores to a healthy condition

currency—paper money and coin of a country

custody—control; care

customs—a government department that collects taxes on imported or exported goods

damage—harm or injury

damages—money paid for injury or harm

dark horse—a person who might win an unexpected victory

dawn—early morning at sunrise

daze—to cause to become confused, especially by a blow to the head

dead heat—equal in some contest; a state of equality

deadline—a time by which something must be finished

deal—an agreement

debate—a meeting where differing views are discussed

debris—what remains of something broken or destroyed

decade—a ten-year period

deception—(from "deceive")—the act of tricking or causing to believe what is not true

decimate—to destroy a great part of

decline—to refuse

decree—to order

de facto—in fact; actual

defamation of character—the injuring of a person's good name without good reason

defect—1. to leave one's own country to live in the country of an enemy   2. to leave a group and join an opposing group   3. a fault or imperfection

defendant—(in a court)—a person who has been accused

defense department—the department of government in charge of the military

defenses—the armed forces protecting an area

deferral—a payment that is postponed to a later time

defiance—an act of disobeying

deficit—the amount of money below a required amount

defraud—to cheat out of a right or property

defy—to refuse to obey

delegate—a representative chosen by members of a local political party

deliberately—intentionally; not by accident

demand—an order that must be obeyed

Democratic party—one of the two major US political parties

demolish—to destroy completely

demonstrate—to publicly express one's opinion, often by marching, carrying signs, etc.

densely—close together; heavily

deny—to claim to be untrue

deplore—to express strong disapproval of

deployment—putting in position ready for use

deposit—a collection of some mineral

deputy—an assistant

desperate—done as a last hope in a dangerous situation

destination—the intended end of a journey

destruction—great damage

detective—a police officer whose job it is to find out information about crimes

detention—imprisonment; a keeping in prison

deteriorate—to worsen

deutschmark—the basic unit of currency in the Federal Republic of Germany (W. Germany)

devastation—destruction

devout—deeply religious

diagnosis—the discovery of the nature of a problem

dictator—a leader who has complete power over a country

diplomat—a person who represents his own country, often in another country

diplomatic—of diplomats

diplomatic relations—formal relations between countries and their leaders and representatives

disarm—1. to get rid of weapons   2. to take weapons away from

disaster—a sudden great misfortune causing great injury or harm

discipline—orderly behavior in accordance with rules

discontented—unhappy; dissatisfied

disgruntled—dissatisfied

disguise—clothing or make-up that changes one's appearance and hides one's true identity

dislodge—to remove from a place

dismantle—to take apart; to take out of use

dispose—to get rid of

dispute—1. a disagreement 2. to disagree with

disruption—a break

dissolve—to dismiss

distort—to change away from the true meaning

distortion—the act of changing in a bad way

ditch—a long narrow area that has been deepened by digging

divert—to change from an intended path

dividend—money paid out of a company's earnings to owners of the company's stock

division—a large army unit

divorce—the ending of a marriage

dogfight—a fight between two or more airplanes

domestic—within one's own country

dormant—not active

double agent—a person who is supposed to gather secrets for one country, but who actually works for another country

doublecross—to misuse a trust and cause injury

Dow Jones Industrial Average—the average of the closing prices of 30 representative stocks traded at the New York Stock Exchange

drama—a time of high excitement and tension

drastic—1. to a great extent 2. unusually strong or violent

drought—very dry weather

drown—to die in the water from lack of air

Drug Enforcement Administration—the government department that ensures that drug laws are obeyed

drug pusher—a person who sells illegal drugs

earthquake—a movement of the earth's surface

economy—the money, industry, and trade of a country

efficient—working well; working effectively; giving good results

elect—having been elected but not yet in power

election—the choosing of a person or persons for a position by vote

electoral college—(in the US)—the group chosen by the people to elect the president and the vice president

electoral vote—the vote by the electoral college

electorate—the total number of people able to vote in an election

elegant—excellent; of the highest quality

eligible—having the right to do something

eliminate—to get rid of; to kill

embargo—a government order forbidding trade with another country

embassy—the official headquarters of one country inside another country

embezzlement—to unlawfully keep money that has been put under your care

emergence—a coming into being or power

emergency—a serious situation requiring immediate action

emphasize—to express the importance of something

employee—a person who works for another for pay

enforcement—the act of ensuring that a rule or law is followed

engulf—to cover completely on all sides

enriched—made finer in quality or purity

enterprise—a business organization

entrepreneur—an employer; a person who runs a business

epicenter—the point directly above the center of an earthquake
erstwhile—former
eruption—the escape of very hot rock and gas through a hole in the earth's surface
established—firmly in existence
estimate—1. to make a rough guess of a number or quantity   2. an approximate number arrived at by guessing
evacuate—to take people away from an area
evidence—something that helps to prove or disprove an accusation or position
ex-convict—a person who has previously been in prison
excavation—the making of a hole by digging
exchange—a place where stocks are bought and sold
execute—1. to put a person to death according to the law   2. to kill   3. to carry out
exit—a way out
exotic—highly unusual
expansion—1. an increase in size   2. growth
explode—to blow up or burst apart
exploitation—1. using for selfish purposes   2. using for profit
explosion—the act of blowing up or bursting apart
export—a good sold to another country
extinguish—to put out (a fire)
extract—to take out of the ground
eyewitness—a person who is present and sees something happen

facility—a building and equipment
faction—a small group within a larger group
famine—a great lack of food
fatality—an accidental death
fatally wound—causing injury that leads to death
favorite son—having the support of one's own state
feasibility study—a study to determine whether something is possible and worthwhile
feat—a success; a clever action
featherbedding—the use of more workers than are necessary to do a job
federal—national
federal reserve—the central banking system of the US
feminist—a person who believes strongly in the rights of women
fictitious—false; not real
fighter interceptor—an airplane, usually small and very fast, that is designed to attack and destroy other aircraft
figure—an important or well-known person
file—to present to a court for action
file for divorce—to ask a court to end a marriage
file suit—to take a noncriminal case to be decided in a court of law
finance—to provide money for
finances—supply of money
financial—concerning money
firm—a business organization
fission—the splitting of the atom
fistfight—a fight using closed hands
fixed—set at a definite level
flag of convenience—the practice whereby a shipowner registers his ships in a country with lax regulations or minimal taxes even though he does not live in the country
flame—the burning gas of a fire
flee—to go away for safety reasons; to escape

fleet—a group of ships, especially warships

focus—to concentrate

forecast—1. to say what one expects to happen   2. a statement of what is expected to happen

foreign minister—the government minister in charge of foreign relations

foreman—the leader of a group of workers

forgo—to not carry out

fortune—great wealth

foul play—criminal activity

foundation—the lowest part of a building

fragile—weak

frantically—excitedly, especially through fear

fraud—an act of deceiving which is usually against the law

free scrip issue—the issue of stock certificates at no charge, usually in place of paying a dividend, to allow the company to keep its cash for investment

freight—goods transported

freight rate—the price of transporting goods

frigate—a warship (larger than a destroyer)

frozen asset—money or property that a court has forbidden to be used

fuel—1. to cause   2. a substance that can be burned, such as wood, coal, or oil

fund—an amount of money for some purpose

fundamentalist—a person who believes strongly in a religion and attempts to follow its teachings very carefully

fusillade—a number of gunshots fired at the same time

fusion—a nuclear reaction in which the nuclei of certain atoms join together

futile—without a chance of success

gang—a group of people working together

gangster—a member of a gang of criminals

gas mask—a device worn over the nose and mouth to protect a person from harmful gases

general—a high-ranking military official

General Assembly—the United Nations body that includes all member nations, each having one vote

generate—1. to cause to be   2. to produce usable energy

geothermal—of the heat from inside the earth

gesture—an action intended for effect

gigantic—very large

give in—to yield; to do what has been ordered

goodwill gesture—an expression of good intentions

governor—the highest official in a US state

grand larceny—the stealing of a large amount of money or property

grant—money given by the government or an institution

grenade—a small bomb

grievance—a wrong; a cause for complaint

grievance procedure—a method for settling a complaint

gross—total

gross national product (GNP)—the total value of all goods and services produced in a country during a period of time

guarantee—a formal promise that something will be done

guarantee a loan—to promise to repay borrowed money for another person in the event that person cannot repay it

guerrilla—a member of a small group of soldiers

guilty—having done a crime or improper action

gust—a sudden strong rush of wind

gut—to destroy the insides of

146

halt—stop
hamper—to make difficult
handcuff—metal rings for holding the hands of a prisoner
harass—to give trouble to
harbor—a protected part of the shore which is deep enough for ships to stop at
hardline—not favoring compromise, especially with one's enemies
harsh—strict and unpleasant
hashish—an illegal drug taken from the tops and leaves of the Indian hemp plant
hastily—quickly
haul—the total amount seized
headquarters—the main offices of an organization
heist—a robbery
helmet—a protective covering for the head
heroin—an illegal drug made from opium
high technology—using modern and advanced production methods
hijacker—a person who takes control of a vehicle, ship, or airplane by force
holding the reins—in control; in power
hold-up—a robbery where force is used
holocaust—a fire causing great loss of life
hospitalize—to put in the hospital
hostage—a person who has been taken prisoner in order to force another person
　　or persons to do something
House Majority Leader—the leader of the majority party in the House of
　　Representatives
House of Commons—the part of the British or Canadian parliaments whose
　　members are chosen by the people to make the laws of the country
House of Representatives—one of the two law-making houses in the US
　　government
hurricane—a violent storm, generally occurring in the warmer regions
hurtle—to move at great speed
hydroelectric—concerning the producing of electrical energy using falling water

identification—information about a person
identify—to recognize as being a particular person
identity—a person's name
ignite—to cause to burn
ignore—to take no notice of
illegal—against the law
illegal immigrant—a person who enters another country unlawfully
illicitly—unlawfully
image—an idea of what a person is like
impact—the hitting of one object against another
imperative—necessary
import—a good brought into a country from another country
impound—to seize and keep under the power of a court
improvise—to do quickly without prior planning
incentive—something that causes action
incident—an event
income tax—a tax on money earned
incredible—seemingly impossible; difficult to believe
incumbent—presently holding a position
indict—to formally accuse of wrongdoing in order to bring to trial in a court of law
indoctrinate—to teach and try to convince
industrialized—having a well-developed economy with large manufacturing
　　organizations
infamous—well known in a bad way

inflammable—able to burn
inflation—a big rise in prices of goods and services
informant—a person who gives information
inhabitant—a person who lives in a place
initial—at the beginning; early
initiative—a step leading to action
injure—to hurt
injustice—a lack of fairness
innocent—having done no wrong; not guilty
innocent bystander—a person who is present at an event but who is not involved
instantly—immediately
insufficient—lacking something necessary; not enough
insurgent—a member of a group fighting against the government
intact—whole
intelligence—concerned with secretly gathering information about other
     countries
intensive—showing great energy or activity
intercept—to stop from going to a particular place
interference—coming into contact with and having a bad effect
interest—a payment for the use of money borrowed
interest rate—the amount of payment for the use of money borrowed, expressed
     as a percentage per unit time
interim dividend—a dividend paid to shareholders part way through the year
interpreter—a person who explains what has been said in one language in terms
     of another
intimidation—the act of controlling a person's actions through fear
inundate—to flood
invade—to enter another country with force
invasion—the act of entering another country with force
investigate—to search for information
investment—the spending of money for something that is expected to earn more
     money
investment credit—reduced taxes to encourage investment
ironically—a result that is opposite to what was expected
irrefutable—that which cannot be disproved
irregularity—an improper action
irrelevant—not important; not related to the main point
irrigation—the supplying of water to land
isolate—to keep away from something
issue—1. to make public   2. a point or matter that is important to the public
     3. the giving of stock certificates, usually to those who already own shares in the
     same company, increasing the number of shares outstanding whether to raise
     more money or as a substitute for dividends

jampacked—completely full
jeopardize—to put in danger
job action—a work slowdown
joint stock enterprise—a business venture in which two or more parties hold
     stock, usually where each party provides certain abilities to make the enterprise
     prosper
joint venture—a business activity involving more than one organization
judgment—a court decision
judicial system—the system of hearing and deciding cases in courts of law
just—fair
justice—fairness

key—of highest importance
kickback—an illegal payment made to a public official who has helped a business win a public contract
kidnapping—the unlawful taking away of a person against that person's will
kingpin—the leader

labor—to work
laboratory—a special building or room in which a scientist works
lackluster—dull; not impressive
ladder—a structure for climbing
landmine—a bomb hidden in the ground
landslide—1. very large   2. a victory by large numbers
launch—to start
lava—the hot fluid rock that comes out of a volcano
law enforcement official—a policeman
layoff—the act of putting workers out of work
leading indicators—a group of economic statistics that often show how an economy will perform in the near future
leak—to go accidentally through a hole or crack
leftist—a supporter of a group that favors the equal division of wealth and property among all
legal—concerning or using the law
legislation—a law or group of laws
legislator—a lawmaker
leisure—free time
lend—to give the use of money with the understanding that it will be paid back
lethal—able to cause death
levee—a wall to prevent a river from flooding
libel—the act of injuring a person's good name in writing or pictures
liberal—favoring change; favoring a strong government role in society
liberate—to set free
license—formal permission to carry on a business
litigation—the hearing of a lawsuit in a court of law
loan—money borrowed with the understanding it will be repaid
lobby—to attempt to persuade a lawmaker to vote in a particular way
lobbyist—a person who attempts to persuade lawmakers to vote in a particular way
local—a local unit of a national union
loot—money or property taken dishonestly
looting—the unlawful taking away of property
lucrative—profitable; capable of earning large amounts of money

magistrate—a minor judge who deals with less serious cases of law
majority—more than 50% of the total
make public—to give information to the public
malfeasance—an unlawful act, especially by a government official
management—the person or persons in control of an organization who make the major decisions
mandate—instruction as to policy
mangle—to crush and put out of normal shape
manslaughter—the unplanned, but unlawful killing of a person
manufacture—to make or produce goods by machinery or by hand
margin—an amount of money above a certain level
marijuana—an illegal drug made from the dried leaves and flowers of the Indian hemp plant

marksmen—people who are very skilled at shooting guns, especially from long distances

Marxist—a supporter of the ideas of Karl Marx; a communist

mass transit—transportation systems, including buses and trains, capable of moving large numbers of people

massacre—the killing of a large number of helpless people

massed armor—tanks and other heavily protected mobile weapons used in large numbers in a small area

massive—very large

mastermind—to plan and direct

materialize—to come into being; to happen

mature—having well-considered ideas

mayor—the highest official in a town or city

measure—an action

media—newspapers, television, and radio

mediation—the process of settling a dispute through the help of an outsider

mediator—a person chosen to help settle a disagreement

medical—of the science of medicine; of health care

megawatt—1,000,000 watts—a unit of electrical power

mercy—a willingness not to punish an enemy or wrongdoer

meteorologist—a person who studies the weather

militant—favoring strong and perhaps violent action

military—concerning the army or armed forces

minister—a person who manages a government department

ministry—a government department headed by a minister

minority—a racial or social group that is smaller in number than the major group in a society

misdemeanor—an unlawful act that is not very serious

misguided—led into error

missile—an explosive flying weapon that can be sent from the ground, from an airplane, or from a ship

mobilize—to make ready for war

mockery of justice—a totally unfair situation

moderate—not extreme; medium

moderation—avoiding extreme action; avoiding complete disagreement

modest—small in amount

molten—made liquid by heat

momentum—an increase in strength; progress

monitor—to watch a situation closely

motive—a reason for doing something

movement—a loosely organized group united for a particular purpose

mudslinging—attempting to destroy the good name of an opposing political candidate

multi-phased—having several steps occurring at different times

multiple—many

municipal—of the government of a town or city

mutual—held equally by two or more persons or groups

narcotic—an unlawful drug, such as heroin or cocaine

National Guard—the military forces of the US government who work within a particular state

nationalized industry—industry that is owned by the government

negative—not favorable

negotiable—that which can be exchanged for money

negotiations—discussions attempting to reach an agreement

net—1. to gain   2. to gain as profit

network—an organization or system
neutral—favoring no particular side in a contest or dispute
nomination—proposal for a political office
nonaligned—favoring no particular side in a contest or dispute; neutral
nonlethal—not able to kill
normalization—the act of bringing to a normal state
nuclear weapon—a weapon using the power of the atom, such as the atomic or hydrogen bombs

obscure—to make difficult to see
observer—a person who watches and studies an area or situation
occupy—to be present in and control
offense—an unlawful act
official—a person who holds an office
on the floor—under consideration by the full lawmaking body
operation—a military activity
opponent—a person who is on the opposite side in a contest; a competitor; a rival
oppose—to be against something
oppressed—suffering under the power of unjust rulers
ordeal—a time of great suffering
organized crime—a group of criminals who work together in some way, often setting up businesses with profits from their criminal activities
oust—to remove from power
outnumbered—fewer in number than an opposing force
overhaul—an improvement
overtake—to catch up to and pass
overthrow—to defeat, especially a government; to forcibly remove from power
overturn—to determine that an earlier decision was incorrect
overwhelm—to be too much or too strong for; to overpower
overwhelmingly—by a great number

package—a complete set
pamphlet—a short piece of writing on some subject over which there is usually disagreement
panel—a group of persons
panic—great fear often affecting a group of people and causing unreasonable action
paralyze—to cause to be unable to function
parched—dry from heat
parity—equality
parliament—a lawmaking body of the type found in Great Britain
parole—the freeing of a person from a prison before the end of the punishment period because of good behavior
party—a group of people united in political opinion and purpose
passively resisting—opposing something without using violence
patient—a sick person under the care of a doctor
pay hike—an increase in pay
payroll—a list of persons to be paid and the amount to be paid
peaceful coexistence—enemies living together peacefully and avoiding war to settle disputes
peasant—a person who works on a small piece of land
peddle—to sell or attempt to sell something
penalty clause—a part of a contract that states what must be done if the contract is not fulfilled
Pentagon—the building that contains most of the US Department of Defense
perish—to be killed

perjury—the telling of a lie in a court of law after one has promised to tell the truth

permanent—for a long time

pessimistic—expecting something bad to happen

petty larceny—minor stealing

picket line—a group of striking workers who stand outside a place of work and try to persuade or prevent others from entering

pickpocket—a person who steals from the pockets of other people

piling—wooden and steel supports for a building

piracy—the robbing of a ship, airplane, or vehicle

pistol—a handgun

pit—a deep hole from which minerals, such as coal or iron, are taken

placard—a written sign

plague—to cause trouble for

plaintiff—a person who brings a complaint to court

plant—the buildings and equipment necessary for an industrial business

platform—the principles and policies of a political party as stated before an election

plea—a request

plead—to answer to a legal accusation by admitting or denying the accusation

pledge—a promise

plot—the plan of a story

plunge—1. to rush   2. to fall at great speed

policy—a plan of action followed or proposed by a government or organization

politician—a person whose business is politics

politics—the science or art of government

poll—an analysis of public opinion by questioning a group of people thought to be representative of the society as a whole

pollster—a person who carries out and analyzes a poll

pollution—impurity; uncleanliness

pontiff—the pope; the leader of the Catholic Church

pope—the leader of the Catholic Church

popular vote—the total vote by the people (as distinguished from the "electoral vote")

portfolio—a collection of stocks owned by an investor or investing institution

post—1. to put in a position   2. a military or police station

pound sterling—the basic unit of money in Great Britain

poverty-stricken—extremely poor

predict—to say what one expects to happen

premier—the chief minister in the government

pressure—strong power or influence

presume—to think

prevent—to stop from happening

primary—an election to choose who will represent a political party in a general election

prime—most important

prime minister—(in the parliamentary system)—the chief minister in the cabinet

priority—that which must be done before all else

private sector—the part of the economy owned by individuals rather than the government

productivity—a measurement of how effectively goods are produced, how much is produced per man hour

profit—money gained above costs

prominent—important and well known

prone—likely to be affected by something

prophet—a person who can speak for God

proponent—a person who is in favor of something

152

propose—to suggest a plan of action

prosecutor—the lawyer who attempts to prove in court that a person accused of a crime is guilty

prospects—the future; the outlook for the future

protection racket—an illegal business where criminals demand money from people to protect them from harm

protectionism—taxing goods from other countries in order to help one's own industries

protest—1. a statement of strong disapproval or dissatisfaction   2. a group of people gathered together to express disapproval

provision—a part of a law

provoke—to cause trouble

purge—a removal from a position

pursue—to follow

pursuit—following in order to capture

put out a contract—to hire someone to kill another person

quake—an earthquake

quarter—three months

quote—to say the exact words of another person

racket—1. a loud noise.   2. an organized activity to gain money unlawfully

radiation—the giving off of radiant energy from a radioactive substance, such as uranium

radical—1. a member of a group that favors great change, especially in a form of government   2. extreme; great

radioactive—giving off radiant energy

raid—a sudden attack in order to seize something

rank and file—ordinary members of a group, not including leaders

rate—the amount of money paid for a service

ratify—to formally approve

ration—a fixed restricted allowance

ravine—a long deep narrow valley

raw material—a material from nature used to make other materials

reactor—a device that can produce a controlled use of atomic energy for electrical power generation

reaffirm—to express continued support

rebel—a person who works or fights against an established government

recession—a time of serious reduction in economic activity

recommend—to suggest

reconciliation—becoming friendly again

recoup—to regain something lost

recover—1. to regain something lost   2. to become strong again

red ink—lost money

referendum—the procedure of having the people of an area or country vote on a particular question

refine—to improve

refinery—a place where raw petroleum is made into various fuels

reformatory—a place where young people who have done something unlawful are kept

refugee—a person who must leave home because of war, a natural disaster, etc.

regain consciousness—to become awake again after a time of being asleep and unaware of one's surroundings

regional—of a particular area

register—to show on a scale

regulation—a rule

reign—the period when a particular leader rules

reinforcements—men and equipment sent to strengthen an existing group

reject—to refuse to accept

release—to set free

relief—1. help for people in difficulty   2. a change for the better

remarkable—unusual

repatriate—to send back to one's own country

replenishable—that which can be used again and again without using up

reporter—a person whose job is to gather news

representative—a person who has been given the power to act for another person or group

repression—firm control, allowing little freedom

republic—a country with an elected head of government, not a king or queen

Republican Party—one of the two major US political parties

reputed—claimed

rescue—to save from difficulty or danger

researcher—a person who does advanced study to find out new facts

reserve—to set apart for a particular use

reserves—that part of the military not in active service but which can be called upon when necessary

resettle—to allow to live in a new place

resident—a person who lives in a place

residential—a part of a town or city where people's houses are, not containing office buildings or factories

resign—to give up an office or position

resistence—forceful opposition

resolution—the formal expression of the opinion or intentions of a group

resolve—to express the intentions of a group

restore—to give back

restrict—to keep within a certain limit

resume—to begin again

resurgence—a return of strength and activity

retail—the sale of a product directly to the final customer

retained profit—the holding back of profits (instead of distributing them to shareholders) in order to expand production or make new investment

retard—to slow down

retreat—1. to move backwards   2. a private residence away from busy areas

returns—election results

reveal—to make public; to give information about

revenge—a punishment or injury done in return for one received

revenue—money earned or collected

revered—much loved and respected

reverse—1. a failure   2. to change and move in the opposite direction

revive—to bring back into existence or use

revival—a return to good condition

revolt—a fight against those in power

revolutionary justice—(in the story "hijack")—to kill under the authority of the revolution against capitalism

Richter Scale—a measure of the power of an earthquake

rifle—to search thoroughly and steal from

ring—a group of people working together, usually for some unlawful purpose

riot—uncontrolled violent activity by a group of people

risk—to take a chance that could result in loss or harm

rival—a competitor; one who wants the same thing as another

role—function; responsibility

rouse—to wake up

rubble—broken pieces of something that once was solid
ruling—a court decision
rumor—a story that may or may not be true
run—to try to win a political office
running mate—one of two people of the same political party who are trying to win two offices that are considered to be interconnected, such as president and vice president
rupture—to break apart
rural—concerning areas away from a city

sabotage—purposeful harming of a building or equipment
safe deposit box—a box kept in a bank where a person can keep valuable things
sagging—moving downward
salary—money paid to a person at certain regular times for work done
sales tax—a tax on goods bought
sampling—a representative part of a larger whole (in the story "Political Campaign," the 5,000 voters are thought to be representative of the country as a whole)
sanction—an action by one or more countries against another country in order to force it to follow international law
satellite—a man-made object put into space to go around the earth, moon, etc.
scab—1. a worker who takes the place of another worker who is on strike   2. a worker who refuses to join a strike
scandal—a disgraceful action that displeases other people
scheme—a plan of action
scorching—very hot
score—to succeed
seal off—to prevent anyone from entering or leaving an area
search warrant—a court order that allows police to enter a place and search it
second degree burn—a serious burn, but not to the extent that skin is destroyed
secretary of state—the head of the US State Department, the department that deals with foreign relations
security—1. under close guard   2. safety
seismologist—a scientist who studies earthquakes
Senate—one of the two law-making bodies in the US government
senator—a member of the US Senate
sentence—to give a punishment
serve a sentence—to spend time in prison
session—1. one of a series of meetings   2. a meeting where business is done
settlement—an agreement
share—1. one unit of stock   2. part
shatter—to break into many pieces
shell—an explosive for firing from large or small guns
shift—the part of the day that a particular group of workers work when a factory is producing 24 hours a day
shock—a sudden strong movement of the earth's surface during an earthquake
shop steward—a union member who represents the workers in a factory
shortage—a lack of something
shoulder—the edge of a road
shrapnel—small pieces of metal from an explosion
single stroke—one action
site—the place where something is or has been located
skid—to slide out of control on a slippery surface
slander—injury to a person's good name through speaking, not writing
slash—to cut
slick operator—a clever worker, especially in a bad way

slogan—a cry or phrase used by a group of people

sluggishness—having little economic growth

smuggle—to secretly bring a product into a country or take a product out of a country without paying taxes

sniper—a man with a gun who shoots from a hidden position or a long distance

soar—to increase rapidly

socialize—to put under the control of the government

solar—of the sun

source—1. a person who gives news   2. a person, place, or thing from which one gets something

spare parts—parts that are used to replace others that are no longer usable

spark—to cause to begin

spectacular—dramatic and exciting

speculate—to form or express opinions without complete proof

speculator—a person who buys and sells stock in the expectation that the market price will soon change

spur—to help to cause

spy—1. watching for secret information   2. to secretly gather information about another country

squad—a small group of people working together

squadron—a group of military aircraft

stability—steadiness; a firm position

stage—1. to carry out   2. the theatre

stampede—to flee in fright

standard—an agreed upon level or rule

standby—able to be used when necessary

starvation—death through lack of food

state visit—a visit to another country at the invitation of that country's government

statistics—facts about a particular subject in number form

status—state or condition; level; position

stave off—to stop from happening; prevent

stem from—to come from

step up—to move more quickly

stiff—strong

stock—a supply of something

strafe—to attack ground positions from the air with machine gun fire

strategic—giving a military advantage

strategic weapon—a weapons system capable of carrying a nuclear bomb (warhead) more than 5,000 kilometers

strategy—a plan of action

strewn—fallen over a surface in separate pieces

strife—a battle or struggle

strike—1. to attack   2. a refusal to work

stronghold—a well-protected place

stun—to confuse or cause to lose consciousness through a shock or blow

stunning—very surprising

submit—to offer for consideration

subside—to go down to a lower level

subsidiary—a company that is controlled by another company

subsidize—to provide money for

subsidy—money provided by the government

substantiate—to show as being true by giving proof

suburb—a town or city at the edge of a much larger city

suburban—of an area immediately outside a town or country

subversion—a purposeful attempt to destroy

successor—a person who takes the place of another

succumb—to yield

sue—to bring a court action against someone because of some harm done

suicide—the act of killing oneself

suit—an action in a court of law brought against another in order to gain a right or property; a noncriminal case in a court of law

sum—an amount of money

summit conference—a meeting of the leaders of countries

superiority—the condition of being greater in amount or quality

superpowers—the major world powers, generally considered to be the US, USSR, Great Britain, France, and the People's Republic of China

supplies—necessary things, such as food and equipment

suppress—forcefully putting an end to some activity

supreme court—the highest court of a country

surge—1. a rapid rise   2. a period of great success

surgeon—a doctor who cuts and removes diseased parts

surgery—the cutting and removal of a diseased part

surplus—that which is more than is needed or used

surrender—the act of giving up or yielding to the power of another

surround—to go on all sides; to encircle

surveillance—a watch kept over a person or place

survey—a general examination of a situation

survive—to continue to live after an event where death was possible

suspect—a person who is believed to have done something wrong

suspend—to stop

suspended sentence—freedom from punishment on the condition a person behaves properly for a certain period

sustain—to support; to grant as correct

swerve—to turn sharply, especially in order to avoid something

swing—a journey

tactical—of military importance

tactical role—the use of a weapon to gain immediate advantage on the battlefield, usually by destroying enemy weapons or soldiers

tactics—the methods of acting in a battle

talent—skill

tally—to count

tank—a vehicle for fighting, covered with heavy metal and armed with heavy weapons

tariff—a tax on goods brought into or sent out of a country

tariff barrier—taxes on foreign goods which make trade difficult

tear gas—a gas that brings water to the eyes and makes them hurt

technicality—a mistake during a trial

temporary—lasting only for a certain period of time; not for all time

tender bid—a proposal to perform a service or provide equipment at a certain price under certain conditions. Usually the party wanting the service or equipment will seek tender bids from a number of companies and choose the best one.

terminal—the part of the airport where passengers come and go

terror—great fear

terrorist—a person who attempts to gain something through fear and threats

testify—to give information in court, promising that the information is true

testimony—a statement sworn to be true, usually given to a court

theft—an act of stealing

theorize—to give a possible explanation for something

thermal—concerning heat

thief—a person who has stolen money

third degree burn—a very serious burn that destroys skin and underlying tissue

threat—1. an expression of an intention to hurt or punish   2. danger

threaten—1. to seem likely to happen, especially something bad   2. to be likely to cause harm to   3. to express the intention to do something harmful

thug—a tough violent criminal

ticket—members of a political party who are running for various political offices at the same time

tidal wave—a very large wave which can cause great damage

tide—the rise and fall of the ocean caused by the pull of the moon and the sun

tight monetary control—careful and effective efforts by government authorities to ensure that the supply of currency in a country grows no more quickly than they want it to

tight money supply—the situation that occurs when the amount of money allowed to be printed and circulated is growing at a slower rate than the economy's need for money

time table—schedule

tip off—to give information

toast—an expression of goodwill given immediately before drinking in honor of a person

toll—the number of people killed

touch off—to set on fire or cause to explode

touch on—to discuss

toxic—poisonous

trace—to discover through investigation; a mark or sign of the presence of a person or thing

trade—the buying and selling of goods and services

trade barrier—something (usually a tax) that makes trade difficult

tragedy—a terrible and unfortunate event

trail—to be behind

transaction—a business activity

transition team—the group of people who plan for the change of administrations

transmit—to send information electrically

trapped—caught; unable to escape

treason—an unlawful act against one's own country

treaty—an agreement between two or more countries

tremor—a shaking of the earth's surface

trend—a general direction or tendency

trespassing—unlawful entry into property owned by another

trial—the hearing and judging of a case in a court of law

tribunal—a court of law

trigger—to cause

triggerman—a man with a gun, especially one who shoots at another person

trooper—a soldier

troops—soldiers

tropical—of the warm wet regions of the earth

truce—an agreement to stop fighting

tumor—an abnormal growth in a part of the body

turmoil—great confusion or disturbance

turning point—the time at which an important and decisive change happens

ultranationalism—blindly looking after one's own country's interests above all else

unconscious—asleep, generally because of injury, illness, or medicine

underworld—the society of people who break the law to earn their livings

undisclosed—not made known

unearth—to discover
unemployment—the condition of not having a job
unforseeable—that which cannot be predicted
unfounded—having no facts in support; untrue
unidentified—unknown as to name or nature
uniform—the same style and color of clothes worn by a group of people
union—an organization of working people
upheaval—a great change
unprecedented—never having happened before
upset—to win an unexpected victory
urban—concerning the city
urge—to persuade strongly
urgent—that which must be done quickly

vast—very large
veer—to turn to another direction
vendetta—a war between families or small groups
verdict—a court decision
verge—(on the verge)—very close to
verify—to confirm to be true
veteran—a person who has been in a war as a soldier
veto—to reject; to refuse to accept
victim—a person who suffers from something harmful
vigorous—active
violation—the breaking of a rule or law
vindication—the act of clearing one's name of suspicion due to a wrongful accusation
violence—strong force intending to injure or damage
vociferous—outspoken; making one's views known at every opportunity
volcano—a hole in the earth's surface that allows the escape of very hot rock and gas
voluntary—having free choice; not forced
volunteer—a person who offers his services freely
vote—1. to choose among possibilities by writing on a piece of paper, raising one's hand, etc.   2. a choice
vote of confidence—(in the parliamentary system)—a vote on an important issue which, if lost by the government party or parties, results in a general election being called
vow—to promise to do something

wage—1. money paid to a worker for work done   2. to carry out
wake—the path of something that has already passed
war-shattered—heavily damaged by war
warehouse—a place where goods are kept for future use
weapons-grade—of high enough quality to be used in a weapon
weather bureau—a government department that gathers information about the weather
welfare system—government help to people in need, especially the poor, the sick and the elderly
wholesale—the sale of a product to someone who will sell it again
widespread—occurring in many places
wildcat strike—a strike that does not have the approval of the union
wind-up—to finish
windfall—unexpected piece of good luck
withdrawal—leaving

witness—a person who is present and sees something
women's liberation—in favor of more rights and better conditions for women
work to rule—following all workrules exactly and therefore working very slowly
workforce—the total number of workers in a company, government, country, etc.
wound—1. to hurt   2. an injury
wrangle—a strong disagreement
wreak havoc—to cause great damage and confusion
wreckage—the remains of something that has been destroyed

Answer Key

PART ONE: A READING COMPREHENSION METHOD

Chapter 1

A. 1. b   2. b   3. c   4. a   5. a   6. c   7. b   8. a
B. 1. b, a, b   2. a, b, b, c   3. c, b, c, c   4. a, a, a

Chapter 2

A.
1. John Stonehouse   was freed, b
2. A woman   was told, b
3. An explosion   ripped apart, a, a
4. Iraq   announced, c
5. A strike   threatened, b
6. The island   has been bought, c
7. Panamanians   returned, c
8. Christopher Boyce   has escaped, c, b

B.
1. Firefighters   found, b
2. fundamentalists   were executed, a
3. Police and officials   sought, a
4. The planeload   was sent, b
5. A Japanese-Chinese   met, a
6. explorers   emerged, a
7. Princess Anne   told, c
8. bands   seized, b
9. Alger Hiss   has filed, a
10. A teenager   has decided, c, c

C.
1. WHAT?   to cut off all electricity
   WHERE?   in the state of Queensland
   WHEN?   yesterday
   RESULT?   leaving its 2.5 million residents in the dark
2. BACKGROUND: the first non-Italian in 450 years to be named pontiff of the 700-million-member church
   WHOM?   58-year-old Polish Cardinal Karol Wojtyla
   AS WHAT?   as pope
3. FROM WHOM?   Rolling Stone singer Mick Jagger
   SOURCE?   according to her lawyer
   FOR WHAT?   for a divorce
4. HOW MUCH?   as much as $30 million
   TO DO WHAT?   to pay
   SOURCE: US Rep. Elizabeth Holzman
   TO WHOM?   to the Hanoi Government
   WHY?   to win permission to flee the country
5. WHEN?   today
   BACKGROUND: amid outraged protests from feminists and politicians who claim it would drive women to backstreet abortionists
   FOR WHAT?   for final debate in the House of Commons

6. WHERE?   on the Columbia River
   BACKGROUND: marking the fourth time in four generations that members of the same family have perished on the river
   SOURCE: relatives said
   HOW?   in a boating accident
7. SOURCE: the Sunday Times said
   HOW?   by hurling himself onto a barbed wire fence
   WHAT?   suicide
   WHEN?   in 1943
   WHERE?   in a Nazi concentration camp
8. WHY?   for breaking the country's strict alcohol laws
   WHERE?   in Saudi Arabia
   SOURCE: the Foreign Office said last night
   TO WHAT?   to 80 lashes in public

D.
1. The Tel Aviv municipal government knocked down the wall around the home of Moshe Dayan.
2. Japan will join the United States in clamping economic sanctions against Iran.
3. The US Senate voted to authorize $75 million to help Nicaragua.
4. Japan plans to develop a missile.
5. Mario Vulcannelli took to the streets.
6. Mayor William Green announced the layoff of 10 percent of the city's workforce.
7. Richard Nixon has bought a house.
8. 17,000 residents were evacuated from southeastern Edmonton.
9. Queen Elizabeth II returned to Britain.
10. The FBI has arranged to introduce a double agent.

E.
1. In the hospital
   That he is the oldest resident of the United States
   breathing
2. To protect 1.5 million dollars
   He stole the money.
   Yes
   He was arrested.
3. 46 years
   Yes
4. To grow human cancer tumors in the laboratory
   Doctors may eventually be able to predict which cancer drugs will be effective with which patients.
5. One
6. The first billion-dollar budget was recommended by the UN General Assembly.
   Less
   Yes
   No
7. The chewing of betel and cigar smoking
   Peasants
   These habits are common among the peasants.
8. For independence
   No
   50,000
9. Police arrested 38 bank presidents and businessmen for participating in a scandal.

10. A legal battle begins in the Singapore high court on March 10.
    A dead man's family and Indonesia's Pertamia Oil Company
    The man's multi-million dollar fortune
11. No
    Thieves
    They stole 4 paintings.
    4
    A Dutch Renaissance painter
12. We don't know. The story reports a rumor, not a fact.
13. A light aircraft pilot
    Over Bass Strait in October
    The father of the pilot
    Jacques Cousteau
14. We don't know.
    Guns and hand grenades
    Six and one-half hours
    Air piracy

Chapter 3

A. 1. Questions answered by the story: a, b, c, f, g

A judge, at the wish of the parents of the boy, identified only as Benjamin C., had a short time earlier signed a court order authorizing doctors to pull the plug out of the machine.

Benjamin had been in a coma since he was injured in a car accident three months ago and doctors said he had irreversible brain damage.

2. Questions answered by the story: d (The story doesn't tell you directly, but you can easily guess that **to commit suicide** means **to kill oneself**.), e, f, h

After drinking half a bottle of gin to get his courage up, Moss walked into the sea at nearby Worthing, but lost his nerve after the water reached his chest.

He returned to his hairdressing shop and wired up a metal chair and twice tried to electrocute himself, but each time he threw the switch a fuse blew. Then he broke a mirror and cut his wrists, but the cuts were ineffective. He tried to hang himself from a stair rail, but the knot let him down.

In a final bid Moss piled up furniture and cushions and set them alight hoping the smoke would suffocate him. But the fire got too hot and he climbed out of a window and went to the Samaritans, a non-profit organization dedicated to helping people with problems.

The Samaritans called his mother who telephoned the police.

Moss pleaded guilty to a charge of arson, was put on probation for three years and ordered to undergo treatment at a psychiatric hospital.

3. There are many ways to word the questions. Here is one possible set:
   a. How close were the two planes to each other?
   b. Why did this happen?
   c. What was the weather like?
   d. What was the name of the other airliner?
   e. How many passengers were on the planes?
   f. Who were the officials mentioned in the story?
   Note that all the preceding questions are answered in the story.

Chicago's aviation commissioner, Thomas Kapsalis, said the two planes, with 261 people aboard, came within 100 feet (30 meters) of each other.

He said air traffic controllers had cleared both airliners to use intersecting runways at O'Hare, the world's busiest airport, at the same time.

A Federal Aviation (FAA) spokesman said the American Airlines plane carrying 121 passengers and seven crew passed "a couple of hundred feet" above a Braniff International Boeing 727 with 133 people aboard.

American Airlines Flight 71 from Newark dropped out of low cloud at about 300 feet (90 meters) to land when the pilot, Captain William Voltz, saw the Braniff plane. Flight 231 to Kansas City, took off apparently without realizing it was involved in a near-miss. Aviation officials define two planes passing within three miles (five km) as a near-miss.

The FAA said it was investigating the incident. FAA officials said four near-misses were reported at O'Hare last year out of 896,810 flights handled by the airport.

4. The governor of the walled fortress prison on San Francisco Bay, G. W. Summer, said he was considering taking disciplinary action against the unidentified guard.

The three prisoners, Forest Tucker, 59, John Waller, 37, and William McGirk, 37, all serving sentences for armed robbery, secretly built a boat while working in a warehouse outside the main prison walls, Summer said.

Thursday they put to sea. A guard looking across the bay saw what he thought was a sinking kayak and called to the men to ask if they needed help. They yelled back: "No, we're okay."

The boat, made of plastic sheets, wood and glass, was later found abandoned. The prisoners had painted on the words "Rub-a-Dub-Dub—Marine Yacht Club"—the name of one of the most exclusive yacht clubs in the area.

5. More than 800 offshore catering employees say they want a basic salary of 600 pounds (US$1,386) every four weeks—two weeks on the rigs and two weeks of shore leave, the usual work schedule in the North Sea.

The catering off-shore trading association has offered kitchen crews 440 pounds ($1,016). A new contract was due July 5.

The strike, which began over the weekend, has hit more than 20 rigs and platforms.

Many non-essential maintenance and engineering staff have been flown ashore in an effort to stretch out food supplies for divers and production men.

6. In a tearful scene at the police station of this beach community, Caroline Thompson—only child of Russell and Rachel Thompson of Duwood, Georgia—was reunited with her parents.

Earlier Monday, the car chase punctuated by bullet fire, ended when a patrolman rammed his car in front of her parents' stolen vehicle.

That ended two days of terror after she was abducted from a Florida parking lot in her parents' car.

Her eyes red-rimmed from crying and her voice cracking with emotion, 34-year-old Mrs. Thompson said, "She's fine. She wanted to have her picture in the newspaper a while back but we didn't know it would be like this."

As the Thompsons left the police station to head back to Daytona Beach, Florida, to continue their vacation, they met neighbors from Georgia. Mrs. Thompson embraced a friend, while Caroline hugged a young playmate.

Caroline, wearing a clean dress and resting her head on her father's shoulder, smiled at reporters when they called her name.

"I would like to make a statement thanking them (the Press) for everything they have done," Mrs. Thompson said.

James Keith Tucker, an 18-year-old parolee from High Point, North Carolina, was taken into custody Monday and charged with the kidnapping.

B. 1. **they** = Thousands of Syrians, Palestinians and Lebanese refugees
it = the Israeli invasion of Lebanon
the demonstrators = thousands of Syrians, Palestinians and Lebanese refugees
2. **they** = a hand and the whole forearm
3. **the boys** = two sons
4. **six of them** = six members of an all-woman pickpocket gang
the detained women = six of the all-woman pickpocket gang
5. **this tiny American trust territory** = Guam
the 30-mile-long Pacific paradise island = Guam
the twisting storm = a gigantic typhoon
6. **the decision** = the UN decision to open a bank account to help poor countries
7. **this** = a third of the people killed in alcohol-related accidents are between the ages of 16 and 24
8. The Philippine National Labor Relations Commission
The Philippine National Labor Relations Commission
Female employees adapting their uniforms to emphasize sex appeal
"No strapless or spaghetti-strapped dresses, no see-through dresses with plunging necklines and definitely no thigh-hugging or highslit skirts."
their = rank and file employees
them = female employees
they = bosses

C. 1. a. 3   b. 4   c. 3   d. 3   e. 3, 4   f. 6, 7
2. a. 2   b. 2   c. 3   d. 3
3. a. 2   b. 2, 3, 4, 5   c. 5, 7   d. 4   e. 5

D. 1. a. It is the worst in 36 years.
b. No, there have been two previous floods this year.
2. a. Isidore Zimmerman was awarded $1 million in damages.
b. Zimmerman was imprisoned in 1938 for murder and sentenced to death. Two hours before he was scheduled to die his sentence was commuted to life imprisonment.
He was released in 1961 after a court threw out his murder conviction. Zimmerman sued for $10 million.
c. It was the largest anyone could recall in New York, and one of the largest in U.S. history.
3. a. It temporarily increases U.S. naval air power in the Mediterranean near the Middle East.
b. They said it was intended to signal the Soviets and the Syrians to back off from any military moves in the Lebanon crisis.
c. They denied them.
d. No. U.S. and Soviet naval strength is close to normal.

Chapter 4

A. 1. beleaguered: A; combat: B
2. fettered: B (Picture the situation in your mind.)
3. skidded: B
4. scoffing: A; embargo: C (Understanding the word "embargo" will help you to understand the word "scoffing.")

5. abdicate: C
6. tavern: B (Note that "tavern" is clearly a place of some kind and it is connected with liquor.)
7. raccoon: C; rabies: C
8. clamped: A ("Curfew" is the key word of the story. If you understand it, you don't really need to look up "clamped.")
9. drastically: A
10. asylum: C

B. 1. c   2. c   3. a   4. d   5. b, a (The key word in this story is "forcibly." The Philippines clearly doesn't want the refugee boat in its waters. Note that "towed" is in passive voice. How do you move a boat that doesn't want to move? You pull it.)   6. b   7. b

C. 1. Doubloon: gold coin
2. Encephalitis: a viral brain disease spread by mosquitoes
3. Pylon: the structure that attaches the engine to the wing
4. Aegyptopithecus Zeoxis: a small ape-like creature which lived 30 million years ago; "connecting ape of Egypt"
5. Hydrogen peroxide: a food additive widely used for pastry; widely used as a bleach or sterilizer for pastry and a variety of fish pastes

D. 1. b   2. d   3. c   4. c   5. a   6. d   7. c   8. a   9. b
10. failing; vision; disease; c; He can see nothing to either side unless he turns his head.

Chapter 5

A. 1. Japan is to rush food and aid to the Khmers.
2. A sleepwalker puts 2 people in the hospital.
3. War games are planned.
4. The Islamic Press is to sue a UK (United Kingdom) TV firm.
5. 600 people are trapped by a fire for 4 hours.
6. Romulo says that big power involvement in Kampuchea is dangerous.
7. Cars and schools are the targets of a new save-oil plan.
8. A woman kills her husband and herself.

B. 1. A dead piglet is not really a gift.
2. The story reports one expert's opinion, not a proven fact.
3. The story talks about the Japanese Government (State) and three drug companies. The comma, therefore, means "and."
4. A prisoner escaped using artificial legs given to him by the government.
5. There is still doubt about the killing in the story.
6. We cannot be sure Stepanov was actually forced back to Russia.
7. The story talks about a future possibility, not an established fact.
8. The cars mentioned in the story might be defective. We still don't know for sure.

C. 1. a.   2. l   3. h   4. j   5. e   6. g   7. d   8. c   9. a
10. i   11. k   12. b   13. f   14. i   15. j

D. 1. c   2. d   3. b   4. a   5. b   6. c

Chapter 6

A. 1. Source: Supporters of Republican candidate Ronald Reagan
Unreliable, because the supporters are unidentified and have a clear interest in discrediting Reagan's opponent.

2. Source: Fidel Castro
   Unreliable, even though the source is named. Castro has a clear interest in attacking the CIA and excusing the action by his navy. His story is difficult to check since the incident happened out at sea and all the people aboard the fishing boat were killed.
3. Source: The Japanese minister of trade and industry
   Completely reliable, because the source is identified and is admitting something against his interests.
4. Source: Singapore Prime Minister Lee Kuan Yew
   Completely reliable, because the source is fully identified and the story will be easily checked since such a call and such a conference must be made publicly.
5. Source: Diplomatic sources
   Probably reliable, because diplomatic sources should know, the story can soon be checked since the conference would be public, but still it cannot be completely reliable since the source is unnamed.
6. Source: Pro-Peking newspapers quoting reliable sources
   Unreliable. Just calling a source reliable does not make it reliable and since these newspapers are pro-Peking, they have a clear interest in discrediting Vietnam. The information could still be true, but we cannot rely on this report.
7. Source: Thai intelligence sources
   Unreliable, because it is unlikely Thai intelligence sources would have such detailed knowledge of what was happening in Haiphong, especially since it was supposed to have happened that very same day. It could still be true, of course, but this report must be regarded as unreliable.
8. Source: His major opponent in next year's elections
   Unreliable, because opponents have a clear interest in saying bad things about each other. In this case the source is identified so it is not completely unreliable. You should read the rest of the story to see what evidence the opponent can produce to support his accusation.
9. Source: The official Vietnam News Agency
   Unreliable, because Vietnam has a clear interest in saying bad things about China with which it has sharp differences, and because the story is difficult to check since no one is allowed near the border.
10. Source: President Leonid Brezhnev
    Reliable, because Brezhnev is quoted by name and it is a matter of public record that could be contradicted by the government of Afghanistan if it wanted to. But since the government of Afghanistan is under the control of the Soviet Union, there is little reason to doubt Brezhnev could compel the Afghan government to sign a treaty. There is no reason for him to have to lie about it.
11. Source: Leonid Brezhnev
    Unreliable—here you just have to know the facts of the story that Soviet troops went into the country and a few hours later the head of the government was killed. It seems unbelievable that they would kill the man who invited them. Since the former leader is dead, it is impossible to check with him.
12. Source: US and European intelligence sources
    Probably reliable, because this kind of source would be in a position to know and they have allowed themselves to be identified somewhat, although not by name. But the information is not completely reliable because there is no way an independent observer could easily check it and because the stories tend to be in the interest of the sources, i.e., in making the Soviet Union appear more aggressive.

Chapter 7

A. The Feature Story
Straight News Versus Feature (Search abandoned for missing Prof vs. Hopes dim for missing archeologist)

The straight news format gives the facts most quickly. Remember, you usually get the story's main points in the first paragraph.

The feature format tells the most about the people's personalities. Features are generally very concerned with "human interest" information.

The straight news format gives a brief summary of the facts of the situation.

1. The first story because it is a straight news story.
2. Alana Reed; paragraph 1
3. Dr. Reed is enthusiastic about his work—so enthusiastic that he couldn't wait for his wife. He was not only intellectually interested in his field, but he enjoyed the physical aspects as well. He returned to this part of Mexico almost every summer. This is personal information giving the reader a better understanding of Dr. Reed's character.
4. No, it wouldn't. This is not really news. Its purpose is to give the reader a picture of the story's setting.
5. He must have gotten his information from a face-to-face interview because he described the hotel room. Note that he used the interview to give a structure to the story, mixing his own words with those of Mrs. Reed. This is a common technique in feature writing.

The Personal Touch (American doctor in Beirut)
1. She is Dr. Ann Worthington; in paragraph 5.
2. The story is about the difficulties that a volunteer doctor finds working in a hospital in war-torn Beirut.
3. The mood is dark and sad about the suffering and problems in the hospital, yet admiring of the doctor for fighting against them.
4. The hospital is gloomy—that is sad; but the doctor has found a diver's watch so she can read it even in the dark—that is hopeful. Her hair is greying and she slumps down, showing that she is not so young and that she is weary. These are sad details perhaps, but ones that also build up admiration for her. The story of the little girl who died of burns is terrible, but it also illustrates that despite all the suffering, the hospital staff has not lost its capacity for feeling.
5. Most people would admire and respect her because she has left a comfortable job and a loving family to help people in Beirut.
6. She is mainly concerned with her patients, not with herself. She has sacrificed a lot, but she says she feels more fulfilled than ever before.

Unusual Subject Matter (Mystical profits in Indonesia)
1. Actually, it is possible. The writer says that "it 'looked' like a typical business meeting." This implies that it really was not a typical meeting.
2. In paragraph 4.
3. Meditation was used to help make business decisions and to hire people.
4. It relaxes and opens the mind. It makes it easier to be objective in judging risks.
5. No.
6. For social and business contacts.
7. The idea of mystic management is similar to western systems of positive thinking.

The Advantage of Length (High technology, low employment)
1. No, it is not.
2. Jane Mathesen's new job situation is typical of the changes caused by the new technology. The writer, therefore, uses her as an interest-catching

example which supports the main points of the article.

3. The trend is for work done by people to be replaced by intelligent machines—the latest technology.
4. It raises productivity and profits. It gives people more leisure.
5. It makes many people lose their jobs.
6. One possibility is that the new technology will create new jobs for people. Another possibility is that it will free people to give service to other people while the machines produce the goods. A third possibility is that it will allow people to work less and enjoy more leisure time.

B. Opinion
The Review (Loving the unlovable)
The play "Andy Capp" is being reviewed. The reviewer's opinion is positive. The writer clearly liked the play.

1. a. Fact   e. Opinion
      b. Opinion   f. Fact
      c. Fact   g. Opinion
      d. Opinion   h. Opinion
2. b. Positive
   d. Positive. To answer this you must consider the review as a whole. Being "short on plot" is not a negative comment for a play of this type where plot is not very important. For a different play, however, this could be a negative statement.
   e. Negative. "Too proper" is a negative idea. If you read the whole sentence, the writer's opinion is very clear: "The small cast works together beautifully, and, with the sole exception of bartender Daniel Moore, who comes across a bit too proper for the 'keep in Andy's local, they are fiercely funny." In other words, everyone except Daniel Moore is fiercely funny.
   g. Positive. "But" is the key word.
   h. Positive. "Into your affections" is the key phrase.

The Column (The Wright side)
1. He generally agrees: "Carl Arling has come pretty close to making the right diagnosis . . . lack of investment.
2. Something bad.
3. Investment credits, government funding for high technology research, a technological skills development program, and revitalizing school science and math programs.
4. Increased federal borrowing, higher taxes, and high inflation.
5. Reduced government interference in business activities, meaning fewer regulations and tax cuts. Government should also stand up to foreign governments and see that trade barriers are reduced.
6. Conservative; he is more conservative than the President.

The Editorial (The President's plan)
1. The problem of how to improve the economy and whether the President's plan for this improvement is a good one.
2. To encourage investment in new technology and make American business more competitive.
3. Liberal Democrats and members of the opposition party, the Republicans.
4. One alternative is for an incomes policy to keep inflation low while federal financing helps rebuild industry protected by tariff barriers. Another alternative is for tax cuts to raise profits and thus encourage more investment while forcing foreign markets to open up.
5. He thinks it is good because it focuses on the development of new technology which is the most important part of the problem.
6. He wants Congress to pass the President's plan without any changes.

Chapter 8

1. Party convention

1. This story does not tell us about the election for president, only about the selection of the candidate for president by one party, the Democratic Party. The election for president will be held later and the Democratic Party candidate is one of those trying to be elected.
2. Carl Arling comes from Colorado.
3. Depointe was made Arling's running mate because Arling selected him. Arling may have selected him, the story suggests, because Depointe's appeal to certain sections of voters balanced the appeal of Arling to other sectors. We can also see from the story that Depointe helped Arling win an easy first ballot victory by releasing the candidates who were pledged to vote for Depointe. It might also be that Depointe's experience in masterminding the economic revival of his state would be useful in the government.
4. Since Arling won six consecutive primary election victories, it would appear likely that most of his support at the convention came from delegates pledged to vote for him according to the primary results.
5. Depointe had control of 600 delegates selected in state party caucuses, party meetings, on the understanding they would support Depointe for presidential candidate. It was up to Depointe whether these candidates would be released to vote for someone else.
6. The ticket will propose policies according to the "planks" of the party platform which was described as liberal on social issues, and conservative on economic matters.

2. Political campaign

1. This story does not tell us about the results of the election for president. It is about the campaign and a poll that was taken.
2. The Republican candidate is Vice President Lawrence Letterman.
3. 40.7%
4. Arling's latest gain in the polls corresponded to bad news about the economy—increases in both the trade deficit and the unemployment rate; the Democrats have criticized the ineffectiveness of the Republican administration; so it seems the economic issue is helping Arling to gain on Letterman.
5. Depointe is important because he gives Arling an advantage in the big cities where he has had success dealing with economic problems. But the article also says that the unspoken issue is how the voters will react to Depointe as the first black candidate for vice president from one of the two major parties.

3. Election result

1. Carl Arling won.
2. Lawrence Letterman was leading at the beginning of the campaign.
3. Arling won 308 out of 538 electoral votes so his percentage of the popular votes was less.
4. The analysts quoted in the story said the worsening economic situation and Letterman's poor performance in a debate with Arling were factors in the defeat.
5. Letterman gained most of his support from rural areas and wealthy suburbs.
6. No, the story says the Democrats regained control of the House of Representatives. Control means having at least a majority of the seats in the House.

4. **Debate in the legislature**
   1. No, it didn't pass yet. It was just about to be voted on by one of the two parts of the US Congress.
   2. In the House of Representatives, the larger of the two houses in the Congress, the US legislature.
   3. Some people oppose the bill because it gives federal subsidies to hospitals which might use the money to perform abortions.
   4. No, it won't. It still must be passed by the Senate and signed by the president.
   5. The opponents want to make amendments to the bill that will change the parts of it they don't like.
   6. The bill is intended to improve the health system in the United States.

5. **Vote of confidence**
   1. No, it won't. The government survived the vote of confidence so it will be able to continue governing without new elections.
   2. Five political parties share in the government through a coalition.
   3. The members of Parliament in Israel.
   4. They wanted him to dissolve Parliament because they disagreed with his decision on peace talks and wanted him to hold general elections so the people could show which position they supported by voting for the various parties.
   5. Yes, it has.

6. **Summit meeting**
   1. President Nikolai Kosenko of the Soviet Union and President Carl Arling of the United States.
   2. No, it was not.
   3. Yes, it did. Analysts quoted in the story said the summit had brought the relations between the United States and the Soviet Union to their best point in 20 years.
   4. The problems are with the people in the US Congress and the Soviet Communist Party who oppose the treaty and do not want it to be ratified.
   5. The treaty sets a step-by-step schedule for the gradual reduction of the number of nuclear missiles held by both sides over a period of 15 years.
   6. The two presidents also discussed ways to reduce the mutual distrust and antagonism in both their countries. It appears, according to conference sources, that the two leaders also discussed new approaches on other disputes such as the Soviet occupation of Afghanistan, the US trade embargo against Cuba, and trade and technical cooperation.
   7. No, the START II treaty will not be legally effective until it has been ratified by the legislatures of both countries, and the story says there is opposition to the ratification.

7. **Political ouster**
   1. He was ousted from his positions of power in the government and Communist Party. A government announcement said he retired to his country home.
   2. The story doesn't say who the new president is, or whether anyone has been named president.
   3. The moderate officials were purged from their positions and 500 were arrested.
   4. Defense Minister Gen. Semyon Radischin and KGB chief Lazar Kaganovich.
   5. Because of a dispute within the party leadership over military defeats in Afghanistan, economic problems, and the START II treaty.
   6. The new leaders are expected to stop the withdrawal from Afghanistan and use tough measures against workers demanding more pay for less work.

8. International conference

1. The movement offered to forgo the development of their own nuclear weapons if the Soviet Union and the United States will speed up reductions in their nuclear arsenals.
2. Four non-aligned countries have nuclear weapons according to the story— Pakistan, India, Egypt, and Argentina.
3. Iran and Iraq.
4. They will set up a mediation panel which will begin work immediately to try to negotiate an end to the war.
5. It appears that it was not, because it has welcomed the withdrawal of the Soviet troops.
6. Cambodia, with its new neutralist government is the latest member to join the movement.

9. State visit

1. Pierre Lemontre is the French head of state; d'Estaing was previously.
2. Yes, it is. Lemontre specifically referred to the French commitment to the alliance.
3. No, not yet. Lemontre has asked him to, and he is considering it.
4. The government of the People's Republic of Palestine.
5. They must improve to counter the growing military strength of Soviet forces in eastern Europe.

Chapter 9

1. Storm

1. Eva.
2. At least four people have died so far, but it is possible that more people will be found dead later because many people were missing.
3. They were piling up the sand bags in levees to try to hold back the rising tides and prevent flooding.
4. The hurricane was moving at about 12 miles per hour.
5. The fastest winds of the hurricane were moving at about 110 miles per hour.
6. The hurricane winds tore roofs off of houses, caused large waves, knocked down power lines, and sent debris flying through the air.

2. After the storm

1. No, it was not completely over because there were still 50-mile-per-hour winds and 25-foot waves, but this was not as bad as the previous day, so it seems that the worst of the storm was over.
2. 179.
3. The hurricane did at least $800 million damage to houses, power poles and lines, and boats.
4. Federal disaster relief funds will help people to rebuild after the storm.
5. They moved in to prevent people from stealing from the abandoned homes and to help with rescue operations.

3. Accident

1. In Colorado, probably not too far from Boulder on a mountain road, but we don't know the exact location.
2. Sixty-seven people, the 17 who were killed and the 50 treated for injuries.
3. The bus and the tractor-trailer truck.
4. The truck skidded into the bus. It was knocked across the shoulder of the road and overturned in a ditch.
5. It appears that nothing happened to the van since it was not hit by either the bus or the truck.
6. The bus was hit by the truck and fell into a steep ravine.

7. It seems that the bus driver was most at fault since he tried to pass the van on a curve in icy conditions. The driver of the van may also have been at fault for not allowing the bus to pass it more easily.

4. **Fire**
   1. The Luxury Hotel in Kensington burned down.
   2. The fire was caused by a canister of inflammable cooking gas that burst into flames in the kitchen of the hotel restaurant.
   3. Some people were delayed because they had to smash their way through a jammed emergency exit, but because it was near the burning restaurant, that exit was all afire, so the guests had to escape through emergency exits in the rear of the hotel.
   4. The story says six people were reported in critical condition from their injuries and this means that they could die. Firemen might also find more bodies in the rubble of the hotel adding to the total of 70 people already confirmed dead.
   5. Almost all of the hotel was burned. The story says that it was "gutted," which means that all of the interior of the hotel was burned.

5. **Earthquake and volcano**
   1. No, it didn't. The earthquake hit a small island.
   2. The earthquake caused the island's volcano to erupt and started a tidal wave in the ocean surrounding the island.
   3. The island is in the Pacific Ocean, 650 miles west of the Mexican mainland.
   4. The tidal waves have made it difficult to reach the island by sea, and the smoke and ash obscuring the island's airfield have made it difficult to get there by plane.
   5. The people on the island face the danger of molten lava flowing from the volcano toward the main village and the danger of aftershocks from the earthquake.
   6. The officials want to evacuate people from the island.

6. **Drought**
   1. The drought began in mid-May. (The story was written in mid-July and it says the drought has been going on for two months.)
   2. The federal government has allocated more than $15 million in emergency funds to help farmers to irrigate their crops.
   3. Rain.
   4. Strong winds could cause damaging dust storms because the soil in the non-irrigated areas is parched (very dry).
   5. High prices caused by the drought will affect all countries that buy grain from the United States, but the most affected will be those that depend on American grain surpluses to make up their own food shortages. If the drought is too bad, there might not be enough of a surplus to help feed those countries.

Chapter 10

1. **Murder**
   1. No, Joey did not kill anyone; he was killed himself.
   2. We don't know for certain because the killers were not caught, but it is likely the killers were professional gunmen who simply dressed as construction workers to get close to Galatro.
   3. Four men were shot, but one of them is still alive.
   4. Yes, he was an underworld leader.
   5. Galatro was set free because eyewitnesses to the killing could not identify him as the one who did it.

2. **Smuggling**
   1. In Los Angeles.
   2. From Southeast Asia, probably from or through Thailand, since the Thai police were reported set to pick up other suspects.
   3. $3 million.
   4. In a shipment of teakwood furniture.
   5. Customs agents first found the drugs in San Francisco when the shipment of furniture came into the country.
   6. A police informant in Thailand tipped them off—told the police about it.

3. **Corruption**
   1. No, it was the former mayor who was arrested.
   2. No, he wasn't. He was charged with various kinds of corruption.
   3. It was named after him because it was built while he was the mayor.
   4. He took money that belonged to the city, state, and federal governments—really the taxpayers and citizens.
   5. Yes, the story says he bribed federal bureaucrats—officials of the national government.

4. **Lawsuit**
   1. We don't know from the story. The $50 million referred to is not the amount of proceeds, but the total amount of claims and damages the various people in the case are asking for.
   2. No, he didn't. He did not make any decision at all—it was an "out-of-court settlement"—meaning the two sides reached agreement on their own.
   3. He is Lotta Love's financial manager.
   4. The court "froze" the assets so no one could sell them or use them.
   5. Money they made from a movie and about the bad things they said against each other.
   6. Yes, they are planning a co-production.

5. **Robbery**
   1. Over $1.3 million in cash, jewels, and negotiable securities.
   2. They used heavy burglar's tools and explosives.
   3. Three.
   4. They used a truck to knock it into a ditch.
   5. They were dazed by the crash and quickly tied up by the robbers.
   6. No, the robbers took the girl's car and forced her to come with them.
   7. She was hit by a "stray" bullet and the story does not say who fired it.
   8. Three.
   9. Two.

6. **Trial**
   1. No, he didn't. He pleaded not guilty.
   2. They both died.
   3. Because police think that D'aile killed the two robbers. They were shot in the back before the police broke into their hideout. They were shot with a .32 calibre gun—the same size that D'aile normally used.
   4. Twenty-two years ago when he was only 14 years old.
   5. Several days after the robbery.
   6. No, but he studied law in prison.
   7. Because the teen-aged girl was taken hostage against her will—that is kidnapping.

7. **Verdict**
   1. No, he was acquitted.
   2. Yes, but there is a chance he may have to go back to prison. The prosecutor has appealed against the decision and it could be changed.

174

3. Because of lack of evidence showing he committed the crime.
4. They did not find the gun. The murder weapon was never found.
5. She said he was in her apartment.
6. No, she didn't.

Chapter 11

1. **Budget**
   1. Income taxes will fall.
   2. Other indirect types of taxes will rise.
   3. Government spending will be cut.
   4. It will keep tighter control on the money supply and allow less money to circulate.
   5. The price of the pound sterling rose compared to the price of the money of other countries.
   6. The labor union leaders did not like the budget because they think it will create unemployment and economic recession.

2. **Economic forecast**
   1. No, it is not. There will be slow growth in the gross national product and rising inflation.
   2. The economy will start to grow in the last three months of the year at a much higher rate.
   3. No, Walter Abel is the chief economic adviser to the president, Carl Arling.
   4. The president plans to restructure the economy by increasing investment in high technology, improving old factory equipment in the heavy industries, and encouraging workers to work harder and better so they produce more.
   5. Abel said the slow growth, the recession, was caused by the administration of the previous president.
   6. He says protectionism avoids the real problem of how to upgrade US industry so it can regain its lost markets.

3. **Stocks**
   1. Yes, the company is doing very well, with higher profits, good dividends, and a stock issue.
   2. No, the profit before taxes was $14 million; the net profit is less—expected to be about $11 million.
   3. Yes, it is issuing more stock to those people who already hold shares.
   4. Since the issue is one for two, the shareholders will get one new share for every two that they already own. So an owner of 100 shares will get 50 more and have a total of 150.
   5. Yes, it will be paying dividends—these are payments to the stockholders based on the amount of stock they own.
   6. Since pre-tax profits were $14 million and net profit is expected to be $11 million, taxes must be about $3 million.

4. **Stock market**
   1. Yes, they did.
   2. In the morning.
   3. Because of rumors that the money supply had dropped enough to allow the Federal Reserve to loosen the controls on money.
   4. Because some stock owners started selling shares to take profits and because different information on the money supply began circulating.
   5. That the stock market would remain stable with well-chosen stocks gaining respectable earnings.

5. **Contracts**
   1. The contracts were awarded for excavation, piling, foundation work, and structural steel supplies for the construction of the Weekly Courthouse Complex.
   2. No, the contracts were won by local companies even though they put in higher bids.
   3. Mayor Weekly said local companies will have higher standards of quality and had more experience of close cooperation with the city so they won the contracts over the lower bids from out-of-town companies.
   4. Then there will be penalties, but the story doesn't say exactly what the penalties will be.
   5. The city is helping by guaranteeing bank loans to the construction companies.

6. **Shipping**
   1. It is about a treaty to allow developing countries to increase their share of the world's shipping business.
   2. It will reserve cargoes on regularly scheduled ocean liners for the shipping companies of the two countries involved in the buying and selling of the goods.
   3. It will help the ship owners of the countries that ship a lot of cargo, but sometimes ship it on vessels belonging to other countries. It will be especially helpful to underdeveloped countries that want to improve their merchant fleets.
   4. The treaty will hurt the shipping cartels that fix freight rates and previously took most of the cargoes. It will also hurt the shipping companies operating under flags of convenience—registering their ships in countries they have little connection with in order to take advantage of lower taxes or less stringent regulations.

7. **Foreign investment**
   1. We don't know. The story doesn't say anything about it.
   2. It is investing because of pressure from the US government and appeals from American labor unions.
   3. Yotata.
   4. Donha.
   5. Yotata.
   6. They say Japanese exports are hurting the US automotive industry, causing hundreds of thousands of people to lose their jobs.

8. **Trade balance**
   1. West Germany bought more.
   2. We don't know because the comparison in the story is made with the same month the previous year, not the previous month.
   3. Yes, it does.
   4. Yes, it did.
   5. The appreciation of the deutschmark made it more expensive for foreigners to buy German goods and easier for Germans to buy foreign goods. This increased the trade deficit.

9. **Loan**
   1. The American automobile maker, Lord Motors, is borrowing the money because it has financial problems and is in danger of going into backruptcy.
   2. 36 European banks.
   3. The US federal government is guaranteeing the loan to prevent Lord workers from being unemployed and to fulfill campaign promises to make

US industry more competitive by helping it to get the money to buy the latest machinery.
4. The loan is for $1.5 billion. Not all of that is in cash, but the article does not say how much is in cash and how much is in the form of interest concessions and deferrals.

Chapter 12

1. Strike

1. No, they voted to end their strike and go back to work.
2. The coal strike caused a nationwide fuel shortage and sparked off violence between workers and guards.
3. The workers won pay increases, safety pledges, and other benefits.
4. The mineowners won agreement that after 30 days of the next strike, the workers and management will submit their dispute to a third party who will arbitrate the settlement, deciding what each side should get.
5. Yes, four workers were killed when mine guards opened fire on a union picket line.
6. The mines will not start producing coal again for at least another week.

2. Wildcat strike

1. Assembly line workers at the Wayne auto plant went out on strike.
2. No, it wasn't. Wildcat strikes are usually unplanned.
3. Because the workers were unhappy over the heat in the plant and plant foremen accused them of deliberately stopping the assembly line.
4. No, the union did not order the strike.
5. There are three conflicting parties: the foremen who represent the management of the plant, the union officials who want the workers to follow their instructions to demonstrate union discipline, and the militant workers who threaten to continue wildcat strikes until something is done about their complaints.

3. Slowdown

1. No, they stopped short of a strike and are on a slowdown.
2. Train services were disrupted because railway workers were doing everything very slowly, making certain to obey every detail of every safety rule.
3. The railroad officials say there are too many unnecessary men working on the trains so they are trying to reduce the numbers.
4. The railway workers are unhappy because it means some of them may lose their jobs.

4. Protest demonstrations

1. The demonstrators are protesting the construction of a nuclear powered generating plant at Huntsbury.
2. No, the police were not able to end the demonstration, which was reported continuing despite the arrests of more than 5,000 people.
3. There were more than 135,000 demonstrators.
4. Police fired the tear gas.
5. Both demonstrators and police had gas masks.
6. No, they did not fight; they only resisted passively.
7. The demonstrators were being arrested in such large numbers that organizers thought they would soon be able to create difficulties for the state judicial system.

Chapter 13

1. Invasion

1. The Iraqi army has crossed the border and thrust into Iran in a major invasion.
2. The Iranian forces were weakened by the political turmoil in Iran. Well-trained and skillful units of troops were withdrawn from the frontlines to suppress rioting in the capital. The military command has been hard hit by political purges and the armed forces have been weakened by assassination and civil strife.
3. The invading Iraqi armed forces are using tanks, long-range artillery, and MiG fighter bombers.
4. The Iraqis are winning the air war because they have more aircraft. The Iranians have only small numbers of planes and those are old.
5. The Iranian military command has been hit by political purges.
6. This is the second time Iraq has invaded Iran.

2. Guerrilla attack

1. Yes, they did.
2. The government spokesman said the guerrillas raided the post because they had lost weapons to the government and wanted to seize replacements from the police post.
3. The guerrillas took 24 assault rifles and 60 boxes of ammunition.
4. They were ambushed by the guerrillas, but pushed through the ambush to help the police.
5. No, they all got through the ambush safely because a mine laid by the terrorists failed to explode.
6. The guerrillas had a camp in the mountainous area across the border in Argentina.
7. The soldiers pursued the fleeing guerrillas while a helicopter gunship shot at them.

3. Refugees

1. The refugees are from Cambodia.
2. Most of them are going back to Cambodia.
3. They fled to Thailand because of war and starvation in Cambodia.
4. They are returning home because a peace agreement and ceasefire has been concluded in Cambodia and the three groups fighting are giving up their weapons to the United Nations forces.
5. Yes, some of them are afraid they will suffer from more fighting and might have to become refugees again.
6. The United Nations High Commissioner for Refugees is making the arrangements.
7. More than 100,000.

4. Nuclear arms race

1. No, it doesn't. According to the report the two countries are about equal—they have parity in nuclear weapons.
2. Yes, it does. The report says the Soviet Union has superiority in conventional weapons.
3. The Soviet Union would because of its non-nuclear superiority.
4. The race in conventional arms.
5. It suggests the missile be adapted to hit concentrations of tanks at long range.
6. It recommended a lightweight missile capable of being carried by a foot soldier, yet able to knock out heavy Soviet tanks.
7. It is too slow; the study says mobilization of the reserves would take six months.

8. That non-nuclear arms be improved and built in larger numbers because dependence on nuclear weapons to deter an enemy with superiority in conventional weapons might leave only the choice between atomic war and surrender.

5. **Hijack**
   1. None of the passengers were killed.
   2. The two hijackers were killed.
   3. The officials said they were afraid the hijackers were going to start shooting the passengers.
   4. They wanted the government to release all "political prisoners."
   5. No, it did not.
   6. The commandos dressed in prison clothing and pretended to be political prisoners released by the government.

Chapter 14

1. **Oil**
   1. The price of oil and oil products will rise because of the relaxation of price controls on domestically produced oil.
   2. He said the nation was becoming overly dependent once again on foreign oil.
   3. He said he will tax the extra profits of the companies to divert money to the federal government.
   4. He said the money would be used to pay for mass transit, to help poor people pay the higher price of energy, and to develop other sources of energy besides oil.
   5. The president said there could be shortages of fuel in the winter if there is not more energy conservation.

2. **Nuclear power**
   1. A nuclear power plant broke down.
   2. The lives of hundreds of thousands of people and the future of nuclear power.
   3. Yes, they have.
   4. The problem that is still furthest from solution is the problem of how to get rid of the radioactive wastes from the nuclear power plants.
   5. The closure of the plants has increased the danger of electrical blackouts— there might not be enough electricity to go around.

3. **The future**
   1. No, it indicates a grim future ahead with many problems.
   2. No, it is not definite. The report said there would be problems without major policy changes, but offered the hope that new policies in a number of areas could help solve some of them.
   3. The major cause is a severe shortage of oil.
   4. It would cause more pollution with unforeseeable effects on the amount of oxygen in the air and might even change the weather.
   5. No, solar energy is clean, but it is too limited, according to the report.
   6. The breeder-reactor will take a long time to perfect and will not be ready to prevent the energy shortages. Another problem is that its end product is very dangerous because it can also be used to make nuclear bombs.
   7. No, there is no single answer—many different measures must be followed at the same time.
   8. The computer was given information that assumed the current patterns of industrial growth would continue into the future.